MUSEUM OF FINE ARTS — LAUSANNE

Architecture
Art

MUSEUM OF FINE ARTS —LAUSANNE

Architecture
Art

Rizzoli Electa

Philip Jodidio

Table of Contents

Preface by Robert Wilson

←
The American stage director
and artist Robert Wilson, photographed
in the Museum of Fine Arts, Lausanne
at the time of the exhibition *Robert Wilson*
Balthus Unfinished (August 29, 2018)

A CRYSTAL CUBE inside AN APPLE a design for a city

OUR COMMUNITIES NEED CENTERS LIKE IN A MEDIEVAL village where the CATHEDRAL was at the CORE OF THE APPLE, a kind of window to the WORLD TO THE UNIVERSE. IT WAS the HIGHEST POINT IN A PUBLIC SQUARE where people congregated RICH OR POOR, AN OPEN DOOR TO PEOPLE OF THE COMMUNITY and to the WORLD AT LARGE. THIS CENTER CAN BE A TRACK TO DISTANT COMMUNITIES. THE MUSÉE CANTONAL des BEAUX-ARTS de LAUSANNE IS a STATION, A PLATFORM WHERE THE DESTINATION OF ALL TRACKS IS CULTURAL.

ESTUDIO BAROZZI VEIGA'S BUILDING is a COUNTERPOINT IN FORM TO THE SURROUNDING ARCHITECTURE. IT IS CLASSICAL architecture, BUILDINGS AND TREES. THE TREE HELPS US SEE THE BUILDING AND THE BUILDING HELPS US SEE THE TREE BECAUSE THEIR FORMS are DIFFERENT.

RECENTLY I DESIGNED an exhibition "BALTHUS UNFINISHED" IN THE UNFINISHED BAROZZI-VEIGA BUILDING. ALTHOUGH THE building is nearing completion, I HOPE THAT it is NEVER

FINISHED AND WILL ALWAYS BE A STATION FOR DIALOG, A PLATFORM to SEE a permanent COLLECTION OF ART BALANCED WITH A SHOWCASE OF NEW AND EMERGING ART, AN AUDITORIUM, A FORUM FOR FREE EXPRESSION WHERE music, dance, text, poetry, OPERA, in the original sense of the word, meaning OPUS are all INCLUSIVE. WHEN PASSING THE BUILDING FROM THE OUTSIDE, ONE SEES A SERIES OF VERTICAL WINDOWS SEPARATED BY VERTICAL PARTITIONS WHICH REMINDS ONE OF A PASSING TRAIN, A POETIC WAY OF RELATING TO THE HISTORY OF THE SITE. THE MUSÉE CANTONAL des BEAUX-ARTS de LAUSANNE IS A FOCAL POINT IN AN URBAN PUBLIC SPACE, A LONGITUDINAL TRAIN, A DIVISION IN A PUBLIC SQUARE, a backdrop drawing people TO A CITY OF URBAN LIFE and CULTURE. DOMINIQUE de MENIL SAID FOR the OPening OF THE MENIL COLLECTION in HOUSTON: "I WANT PEOPLE TO COME to MY MUSEUM AND LOSE THEIR HEADS."

It IS tHIS THAT it IS
It IS tHIS THAT it IS
It IS tHAt WE SEE AND HEAR

IT IS THAT THAT IS IN US THAT WE MAKE
IT IS a forum with NO ANSWERS
IT IS THAT THAT MAKES us ASK questions
IT IS THAT IT IS AND THAT IS THAT
IT IS THAT IT IS THAT IS IS THAT?

ROBERT WILSON 3.3.19 BERLIN

From Lousonna to Lausanne

Lausanne is an unexpected city, perched on a steep hillside overlooking Lac Léman (Lake Geneva). Archeologists have found traces of hearths and carved flint near the lake at Vidy that are 8,000 years old. More than 200 graves found near the lake date from between 4300 and 3300 BC, attesting to the presence of villages nearby. The same area, near Vidy, was later the location of a Roman military camp. Called Lousonna, it was built on the site of a Celtic Helvetian settlement, after the victory of Julius Caesar at Bibracte (58 BC). The Romans remained in the area until the beginning of the fifth century AD when western Switzerland came under Burgundian influence. The dominance of the Germanic Allamani tribes to the east explains the linguistic division of the country that still exists today.

Not long after the eclipse of the Romans, the town became an episcopate at the end of the sixth century, presided over as of 1011 by a prince-bishop of the Holy Roman Empire supported by the kings of Burgundy. By the thirteenth century, Lausanne had approximately 9,000 inhabitants. The largest Gothic cathedral in Switzerland was consecrated there on October 20, 1275, by Pope Gregory X in the presence of Emperor Rudolf of Habsburg and remains today in slightly altered form in its original location. The Protestant Reformation in Switzerland began to take hold in Zurich under the leadership of Huldrych Zwingli in the 1520s, with Bern following in 1528. Bern, which signed alliances with Lausanne (1525) and Geneva (1526), embarked on an expansionist policy that led them to occupy Vaud in 1536, imposing Protestantism as the local religion and making the Cathedral Protestant. In the same year the forces of the Reformation and the Bernese army stripped the Cathedral of most of its decoration, including altars, statues, and paintings. Certain elements, such as the magnificent rose window (1231–35) and the so-called Painted Portal restored in 2014, both on the south side of the edifice, retain something of the splendor of the original building. The conversion of Lausanne and its Cathedral to Protestantism is more than a matter of historical detail. The austerity imposed by the Bernese and the continuing Protestantism of the Canton are an important element in understanding contemporary choices and the appearance of architecture in the city.

After 1536, Catholic authorities were made to flee, and it was in 1613 that Fribourg became the seat of the bishop of Lausanne. Fribourg is still the seat of the Diocese of Lausanne, Geneva, and Fribourg, underlining the lasting conversion to Protestantism of Lausanne. Subsequent to the Revocation of the Edict of Nantes (1685), Lausanne and Geneva were places of refuge for the French Huguenots, and a seminary created by Antoine Court and Benjamin Du Plan in 1729 was active until 1808. In the context of revolt against the long domination of Bern, Lausanne became the capital of the Canton du Léman also known as the Pays de Vaud in 1798, as part of the République Hélvétique created by Napoleon Bonaparte. Vaud became part of the Swiss Confederation on April 14, 1803.

Particularly since the eighteenth century, Lausanne has been a place of predilection for a number of important cultural figures. Jean-Jacques Rousseau lived in the city from July to November 1730, while Voltaire sojourned at Montriond and Grand-Chêne between 1755 and 1759. Edward Gibbon, author of *The History of the Decline and Fall of the Roman Empire*, completed his opus in Lausanne between 1783 and 1787. Percy Bysshe Shelley and George Gordon, Lord Byron came to Lausanne during a tour of the lake in June 1816, and Byron wrote the poem “The Prisoner of Chillon” at the Hôtel de l’Ancre (now Hôtel et Residence d’Angleterre) in Ouchy, on June 28. The Cathedral was the reason for the presence in Lausanne of Eugène Viollet-le-Duc, who was commissioned by the Conseil d’Etat Vaudois to restore the edifice in 1873. Still working on the project, he died in Lausanne in 1879.

A Brief History of the Museum of Fine Arts, Lausanne

The Arlaud Museum (1841)

Born in Orbe, Switzerland, in 1772, Marc-Louis Arlaud was a portrait painter, the first director of the Ecole cantonale vaudoise de dessin (1822), and the donor, founder, and first director of the Musée Arlaud, the first fine arts museum in the Canton of Vaud, located in Lausanne (1841).

←
Marc-Louis Arlaud
Self-Portrait, 1837
Oil on canvas
60 x 49.5 cm (23.6 x 19.5 inches)

Having taken up the art of miniature portraits with his cousins Louis-Ami Arlaud-Jurine and Jérémie Arlaud in Geneva, Marc-Louis Arlaud moved to Paris in 1797, where he worked first in the atelier of Antoine Louis Romanet, and then, two years later, with the noted artist Jacques-Louis David (1748–1825). David, who had been a supporter of the French Revolution, went on to paint such celebrated Napoleonic works as *Le Premier Consul franchissant les Alpes au col du Grand Saint-Bernard* ("Napoleon Crossing the Alps," 1801) and *Le couronnement de l'Empereur et de l'Impératrice, 2 décembre 1804* ("The Coronation of Napoleon," 1807). Arlaud, still working in the atelier of David, was expelled from France in 1811 for a "crime of opinion" concerning the regime of the emperor. The artist returned to Lausanne and created his own studio and taught drawing. Marc-Louis Arlaud was named director of a new school for drawing by the Académie de Lausanne on December 10, 1822, a position that he held until his death. In 1834 he made a donation of 34,000 francs to the city and in return became the first curator of the Musée Arlaud, built by the architect Louis Wenger (1809–61). The new building, completed in 1841 in a relatively austere Neoclassical style, also housed the drawing school. It was located at the edge of the emerging Place de la Riponne, a market space formerly crossed by the valley of the Louve stream. First imagined by Isaac Augustin Joseph in 1811, the square was actually created in 1838, three years before the completion of the Musée Arlaud. In its early years, the Museum had only works by Arlaud himself and the 1816 donation of the estate of the "pre-romantic" landscape painter and watercolor artist Abraham-Louis-Rodolphe Ducros (1748–1810). At his death in 1845, Arlaud left a sum of 2,500 francs to the government of Vaud for the commission of a painting by the Swiss artist Charles Gleyre to represent Major Davel, who sought, beginning in 1720, to liberate Vaud from the domination of Bern and who was beheaded at Vidy on April 24, 1723.

→

Friedrich von Martens
Place de la Riponne
and the Arlaud Museum, c. 1850
Etching
12.1 x 17.3 cm (4.7 x 6.8 inches)

The Palais de Rumine (1906)

Located on the eastern side of the Place de la Riponne at the base of the hill where the city's Cathedral (1275) and the former Académie de Lausanne (1587), the forerunner of today's University of Lausanne (UNIL), are located, the Palais de Rumine was built between 1891 and 1906 as planned by the architect Gaspard André.

←

Gaspard André
Design for the main entrance of the Palais de Rumine, 1890
Drawing and watercolor
100 x 100 cm (39.4 x 39.4 inches)

The Palais de Rumine was designed to house the city's university, the library of the Canton, and several art and science museums. The Florentine Renaissance style of the building is without any clear relation to local tradition but was thought appropriate in terms of references to a time of cultural renewal and humanism. Article 22 of the Swiss Constitution of 1848 called for the creation of a polytechnic institute and a Federal university. The first of these institutions was established in Zurich in 1854 (ETH Zurich) and, although the second was never created, the idea of housing a Federal university stirred rival ambitions in cities such as Geneva and Lausanne.

It was in this atmosphere that Lausanne received an unexpected donation of 1.5 million francs from Gabriel de Rumine, the scion of a Russian family, born in Lausanne in 1841. The donation was to be invested and spent fifteen years after Rumine's untimely death in 1871. An agreement between the Canton and the city of Lausanne led to the selection of the site and an architectural competition was launched in September 1889. The decidedly heterogenous scheme called not only for a museum of art and new spaces for the library and future university, but also collections of zoology, botany, geology, and paleontology, as well as laboratories, workshops, and offices. Thirty-six projects were submitted and, in an atmosphere of complex disagreement, the second-place project of Gaspard André was chosen in 1890. Born in 1840 in Lyon of a Swiss father, he had already designed the Théâtre des Célestins in his native city.

The essentially rectangular complex, with the long axis on a north-south orientation, was the object of disputes from the outset. Formerly the site of a Dominican convent and blocked on the east by the hill of the old city, the location received little sunlight, and offered few possibilities for future enlargement, in part because of the presence on the Place de la Riponne of the Grenette, a grain market. Because of this and political issues, ten years went by between the first studies for the building and the beginning of construction. Matters were further complicated by the death of the architect in 1896. A team of local architects was named to carry out the plans. Although the University, the Library, and the Museum were able to move into the building in 1904, the official inauguration occurred only on November 3, 1906. As it had been earlier in the process, the rather sumptuous Italianate design was criticized locally because it did not adhere to the relative Calvinist austerity that was prevalent in the region.

The Library and Museum of Fine Arts were placed in basically symmetrical wings on either side of the central "Aula." As of the opening, the building was considered insufficient for its numerous occupants, including the University, which had increased from 600 students in 1896 to 1,200 in 1906. The idea of a single complex housing several institutions certainly had period references in the form of the Augustinergasse museum in Basel (1849, now the Natural History Museum), and perhaps more significantly for Lausanne, the Musée-bibliothèque in Grenoble (1870) designed by one of Gaspard André's former professors, the Parisian architect Charles-Auguste Questel (1807–88). The Museum of Fine Arts had a total of ten galleries on the second floor of the north wing of the building at the time of the official opening in 1906, which were immediately judged insufficient to house both the permanent collection and temporary exhibitions.

The Museum of Fine Arts, housed in the Musée Arlaud until 1904, was directed by Emile Bonjour between 1894 and the end of 1935. For the opening to the public of the Palais de Rumine in July 1906, three large salons with overhead natural lighting exhibited works by Marc-Louis Arlaud, older Swiss and foreign works, Swiss contemporary art, as well as paintings by Charles Gleyre and local artists. Spaces were also reserved to sculptures and drawings. No temporary exhibitions were organized during the tenure of Emile Bonjour. These were held in the Musée Arlaud and in the Grenette until its demolition in 1933. The *VIIIe exposition national des Beaux-Arts* (Eighth Swiss National Exhibition of Fine Arts) was, however, held in the rooms of the Palais de Rumine before the official inauguration. Forty-six thousand visitors viewed this exhibition held between August 20 and October 20, 1904.

The first temporary exhibitions of art in the Palais de Rumine subsequent to the 1906 opening were held in 1938, and by 1942[1] these events were tending to replace presentations of the permanent collections. Temporary exhibitions were visited by 50,000 people in 1946. A show on *Treasures of Venetian Art* drew over 60,000 visitors in 1947. The same year a new gallery located in the lower base of the Palais de Rumine was added to the exhibition areas of the Museum. Despite the emphasis placed on temporary exhibitions after 1938, the Museum had accepted a number of donations that carried requirements that works be permanently exhibited. This was the case of paintings given in 1903 by the family of the Lausanne artist Emile David (1824–91) and of the Widmer collection, promised in 1924 and given in 1936 and 1939.

[1] Information about exhibitions comes from *1906-2006–Cent ans d'expositions au Musée cantonal des Beaux-Arts de Lausanne,* Les Cahiers du Musée des Beaux-Arts de Lausanne, 2007.

↑

Gaspard André
Taureau Farnèse
Project for the Palais de Rumine, 1890
Drawing and watercolor
53.5 x 82 cm (21 x 32.3 inches)

From Ducros to Gleyre

As of 2014, the collections of the Museum included 10,000 works, concentrated in the period between the late eighteenth century and the early twentieth century, with more recent additions including numerous modern and contemporary works. The core of the collection was formed around the work of five important figures. The first of these, already referred to in the context of the Arlaud Museum, is that of Abraham-Louis-Rodolphe Ducros, whose collection was purchased through a public subscription in 1811 and became the property of the Canton in 1816. Works by Ducros in the Museum include his *Sicile. Orage nocturne à Cefalù* ("Sicily. Evening Storm at Cefalù," *c.* 1800–05).

Charles Gleyre (1806–74) was born in Chevilly near Lausanne but was brought up by an uncle in Lyon. He first studied art there before attending the Ecole des Beaux-Arts in Paris. He also studied watercolor at the Académie Suisse in Paris under the English artist Richard Parkes Bonnington, and went to Italy where he met Horace Vernet. After travels to Greece and the Middle East between 1834 and 1838, Gleyre returned to Paris and opened his own studio on Rue de l'Université, before taking over the studio of Paul Delaroche, the son-in-law of Vernet, in 1843. Delaroche had created one of the most important teaching ateliers in Paris and also taught at the Ecole des Beaux-Arts, where, as of 1839, he encouraged students to use the daguerreotype photography process to study painting. It is no coincidence that his students in painting included Gustave Le Gray, Charles Nègre, and Henri Le Secq, who went on to become three of the pioneers of photography. It was perhaps in the context of the atelier that Gleyre had the most influence. Among his students there were James McNeill Whistler, Claude Monet, Auguste Renoir, Alfred Sisley, and Frédéric Bazille.

←

Abraham-Louis-Rodolphe Ducros
Sicile. Orage nocturne à Cefalù
(Sicily. Evening Storm at Cefalù), *c.* 1800–05
Watercolor, gouache, and oil on paper pasted on canvas
96 x 74 cm (37.8 x 29.1 inches)

Gleyre's scene representing the execution of Major Davel, commissioned in the will of Marc-Louis Arlaud, was completed in 1850 and was in the collection of the Museum until it was destroyed by an arsonist in 1980. The painting was such a success that the Canton commissioned a second work, still in the Museum collection, *Les Romains passant sous le joug* ("Romans Under the Yoke," 1858), a subject chosen by the artist himself. The commitment of the Museum to the work of Gleyre has continued into recent years, with exhibitions in 1975 and 2006, and the purchase of a major work by the artist, *La Danse des Bacchantes* ("The Dance of the Bacchantes," 1849). Exhibited at the Salon de Paris in 1849, the work was acquired by Francisco de Borbón (1822–1902), King Consort of Spain, formerly the Duke of Cádiz. Gleyre's painting draws some inspiration from the *Bacchanale of the Andrians* by Titian (1523–26, Prado Museum), as attested by the drawing *Etude pour La Danse des Bacchantes (bacchante couchée)* ("Study for the Dance of the Bacchantes–Reclining Bacchante," 1848–49), purchased by the Museum in 1908. The position of Gleyre's reclining nude is slightly different than that of Titian's weary reveler, but the affiliation is clear.

→

Charles Gleyre
Esquisse pour L'Exécution du Major Davel
(Sketch for The Execution of Major Davel), 1847–48
Oil on canvas
40 x 32 cm (15.7 x 12.6 inches)

→ →

Charles Gleyre
Étude pour La Danse des bacchantes (bacchante couchée)
(Study for The Dance of the Bacchantes–Reclining Bacchante), 1848–49
Black pencil on paper
27.7 x 44.5 cm (10.9 x 17.5 inches)

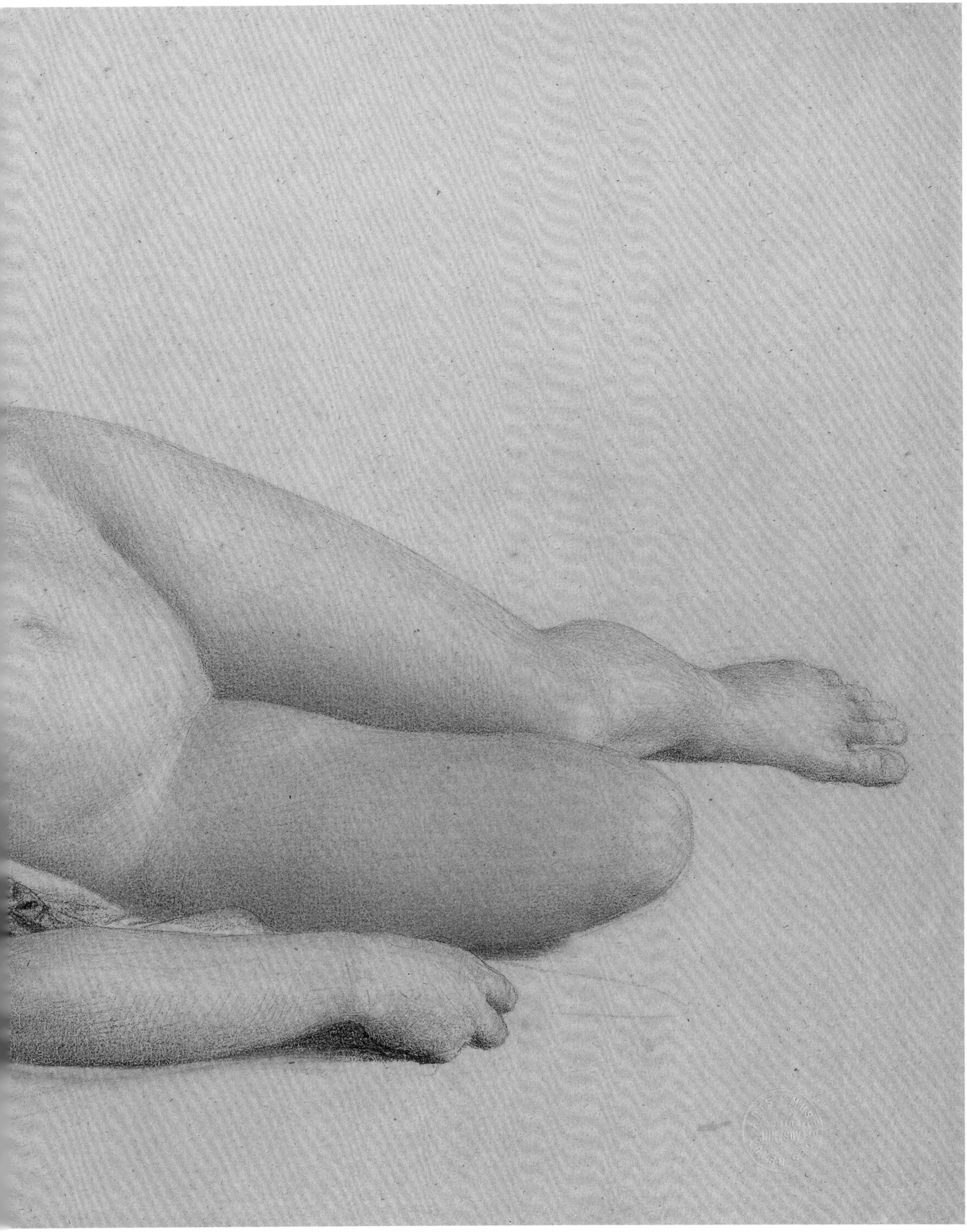

Steinlen and Vallotton

Born in 1859 in Lausanne, Théophile-Alexandre Steinlen (1859–1923) was an illustrator, painter, and sculptor who participated in the Paris circle of the cabaret and publication *Le Chat Noir* between 1882 and 1887. There he was in contact with Henri de Toulouse-Lautrec and Félix Vallotton, but also with Paul Verlaine and Aristide Bruant, the singer and comedian represented by Toulouse-Lautrec in several posters wearing his famous red scarf and black cape. Steinlen also worked with the literary periodical *Gil Blas* and the left-leaning weekly satirical magazine *L'assiette au beurre*. Steinlen illustrated works by Emile Zola and Anatole France among others and is known to have created at least seventy-six posters. The Museum organized a retrospective exhibition of the work of Steinlen between December 1970 and February 1971 in collaboration with the museum of Charleroi and the Basel Kunsthalle. Works in the Museum collection include an 1886 painting *Fortifs* (oil on cardboard, 25.5 × 35 cm) acquired in 1903; a powerful portrait of the Marxist writer Maxime Gorky, *Maxime Gorki de face* (1905, lithograph, 96.7 × 69.5 cm), purchased in 2008; a later large painting *Masséida et le singe Gaspard* (after 1911, oil on canvas), an anonymous 1954 gift to the Museum; and an 1890 poster for a ballet *Le Rêve* ("The Dream," 82 × 63.1 cm), purchased in 2008.

←
Charles Gleyre
La Danse des bacchantes (The Dance of the Bacchantes), 1849
Oil on canvas
147 x 243 cm (57.9 x 95.7 inches)

→
Théophile-Alexandre Steinlen
Étude de chat. Carnet Sources-Croquis
(Study of a Cat. Carnet Sources-Croquis), c. 1902
Charcoal on paper
27 x 20.5 cm (10.6 x 8.1 inches)

Félix Vallotton was born in 1865 in Lausanne and died in 1925 near Paris. He left Switzerland for Paris in 1881 and enrolled in the Académie Julian. He joined the Nabis group in 1893 and was a founding member of the Salon d'Automne in Paris. His work is sometimes described as morose or melancholy, and he did not shy away from unusual modern perspectives or uses of shadow and color, as exemplified in his paintings *Quatre Torses* ("Four Torsos," 1916, oil on canvas, 92 × 72.5 cm) and *La chaste Suzanne* ("Chaste Suzanne," 1922, oil on canvas, 54 × 73 cm), both in the Lausanne collections. Vallotton was an illustrator of the literary and artistic monthly *La Revue Blanche*, which was based in Paris between 1891 and 1903, along with Toulouse-Lautrec (1894), Bonnard (1895), and others. Here the pioneering arts and literature of the time came together with texts by the likes of Mallarmé, Proust, Gide, Claudel, and Apollinaire. Vallotton married Gabrielle Rodrigues-Henriques (née Bernheim) in 1899. Through this family connection, his brother Paul opened a branch of the Bernheim-Jeune gallery in Lausanne in 1913, where his works were sold, in particular to the Winterthur collectors Hedy and Arthur Hahnloser. The Museum of Fine Arts, Lausanne was a trail-blazer insofar as official recognition of the artist is concerned, having purchased his *Autoportrait à l'âge de 20 ans* ("Self-Portrait at the Age of Twenty," 1885) in 1886. Today the Museum has the largest holdings in the world of works by Félix Vallotton, including fifty-six paintings, 300 prints, and 200 drawings. The Félix Vallotton Foundation, based in Lausanne, became part of the Museum with the opening of the new building in 2019, assuring that the institution will be considered the paramount authority on the work of the painter.

→

Félix Vallotton
La Paresse (Laziness), 1896
Wood-block print on paper, no. 18
(one of approximately 180 prints)
25 x 32.5 cm (9.8 x 12.8 inches)

LA PARESSE
FV

←

Félix Vallotton
La Chambre rouge (The Red Room), 1898
Tempera on cardboard
50 x 68.5 cm (19.7 x 26.9 inches)

The Case of Louis Soutter

Another of the significant groups of works in the Museum is that of Louis Soutter (1871–1942). Soutter was born in Morges, near Lausanne, and followed an unusual path, at first studying engineering at the University of Lausanne, but then becoming interested in music, attending the Royal Conservatory in Brussels, before moving back to Lausanne and then on to Geneva and Paris to follow up on a new interest in painting. In 1897 he moved to Colorado Springs in the United States where he became the head of the Fine Arts Department at Colorado College. Returning to Switzerland, he faced increasing mental and physical health issues, but obtained the position of first violin with the Orchestre du Théâtre de Genève. Placed in a hospice in Ballaigues in 1923 because of mental difficulties, Soutter worked, first with pen and pencil and then directly with his fingers, using paint and ink. The architect Le Corbusier, who was a cousin, came to visit Soutter at the hospice after 1927 and began to collect his drawings in large numbers. Le Corbusier wrote about Soutter in the Surrealist magazine *Minotaure* (no. 9, 1936) and helped to organize exhibitions in Lausanne (1937) and New York (1939). Soutter worked in a style that Jean Dubuffet, who discovered his work in 1945 three years after his death, called Art Brut, also today known as Outsider Art. Though any classification of his work related to mental illness is disputed, it is known that Soutter had an influence on such contemporary artists as Julian Schnabel. The Museum organized the first retrospective of Soutter's work in 1961 and another show, *Louis Soutter et les modernes*, in 2003 in collaboration with the Collection d'Art Brut (Lausanne), and has approximately 630 of his works, including several of his Finger Paintings, such as *Souplesse* ("Suppleness," 1939).

In its unusual building, the Museum of Fine Arts, Lausanne traced a path that differs somewhat from that of other institutions that have privileged the art of their own region and country. With artists such as Steinlen, Vallotton, and Soutter, the Museum underlines the importance of painters or draftsmen, born nearby, who moved in the circles that formed modern art, without necessarily emerging as primary figures. These figures gravitated toward Paris and other cities, but along their ways, in different fashions, came into contact with many of the most significant figures of emerging modern art. In a sense, the Museum of Fine Arts, Lausanne offers a slightly shifted vision of the development of modernity, and in this it is an important institution. In 1961, Hermann Hesse, winner of the 1946 Nobel Prize in Literature wrote an unrhymed poem called "Louis Soutter" in the voice of the artist:

I paint
[...]
Not correctly, not beautifully,
but the way things are.
I paint in ink and blood, I paint in truth.
Truth is terrifying.
But I cover my sheet, stroke by stroke,
More loosely, more dense,
gray, silver, black.
I allow the hieroglyph's features
To grow untrimmed, like wool, like moss,
[...]
Sometimes I forget, sometimes
I bracket fear,
[...]
I know, behind my back,
That one, standing and laughing.
He knows me, he knows.

Hermann Hesse, "Louis Soutter," 1961

Souplesse

←

Louis Soutter
Souplesse (Suppleness), 1939
Gouache and shoe polish on paper
44 x 58 cm (17.3 x 22.8 inches)

→
Ai Wei Wei
Dragon in Progress, 2013
Bamboo, silk, and Xuan rice paper
250 x 250 x 180 cm (98.4 x 98.4 x 70.8 inches)

Looking to the Future—Modern and Contemporary

In a sense, the "original sin" of the Palais de Rumine, beyond any aesthetic criticism, was the fundamental lack of space as compared to the number of institutions housed there. As early as 1924, on the occasion of the promised donation of the Widmer collection, the director of the Museum, Emile Bonjour, pleaded for the creation of an independent building that would bring Lausanne up to the standards of other Swiss cities like Geneva, Neuchâtel, Bern, and Winterthur. Significant work undertaken in the building in 1946 resulted in the removal of the sculpture galleries. Further renovations carried out in the 1990s led the Conseil d'Etat to decide in 1991 that the Museum of Fine Arts should be placed elsewhere.

Although the Museum of Fine Arts, Lausanne has continued to purchase and defend the work of local artists, in the period between 1990 and 2010 a greater focus was placed on the acquisition of works by foreign artists such as Christian Boltanski, Sophie Calle, Arnulf Rainer, Marcel Broodthaers, and Luciano Castelli. The director between 1991 and 2000 was Jörg Zutter from Solothurn, who had previously organized shows on the work of Boltanski, Bruce Nauman, and Julian Schnabel in 1989 and 1990 in Basel. In Lausanne, he confirmed many of the strong points of the institution, organizing shows on Vallotton (1992) and Louis Ducros (1998), but also on Bill Viola (1993) and Sophie Calle (1994).

Although Jörg Zutter had been chosen when the idea of moving the Museum was already confirmed, he did not participate in a 1999 commission established to examine future locations for the institution. After examining sixteen potential sites, the commission gave its conclusions in 2000. A location on the shore of Lac Léman at Bellerive was formally selected by the Conseil d'Etat in January 2001 just as Zutter left his position. His successor, Yves Aupetittallot (2001–06) used the galleries in the Palais de Rumine essentially for temporary exhibitions, in the perspective of a new museum to be built at Bellerive. He, too, made use of the permanent collections with shows on Soutter, Vallotton (2002), and Gleyre (2006), while simultaneously welcoming international figures such as Ellsworth Kelly (2002) or Albert Oehlen (2004). Bernard Fibicher evokes the exhibitions he organized as director of the Museum beginning in 2007 in an interview elsewhere in this volume. The final exhibition of the Museum in the Palais de Rumine was organized by Bernard Fibicher with the Chinese dissident artist Ai Wei Wei between September 2017 and January 2018.

Twelve Works

Selected by Bernard Fibicher, director of the Museum, twelve works of art—including paintings, sculptures, and mixed-media—give an overview of the breadth and strengths of the collection, ranging from the eighteenth century to the present.

→

Jacques Sablet
Portrait de famille avec le Colisée
(Family Portrait with the Colosseum), 1791
Oil on canvas
60 x 72 cm (23.6 x 28.3 inches)

↓

Auguste Rodin
L'Homme au serpent
(The Man with a Serpent), 1885 (cast: 1887)
Bronze, brown patina
69.5 x 55 x 29 cm (27.4 x 21.6 x 11.4 inches)

↓

Ferdinand Hodler
Blick ins Unendliche III
(Look into the Infinite III), 1903–04
Oil on canvas
100 x 80 cm (39.4 x 31.5 inches)

→

Ferdinand Hodler
Le Lac Léman vu de Chexbres
(Lake Geneva Seen from Chexbres), 1904
Oil on canvas
70.5 x 108.3 cm (27.6 x 42.6 inches)

F. Hodler 1904

↓

Ernest Biéler
L'Eau mystérieuse (The Mysterious Water), 1911
Tempera on paper pasted on canvas
146.3 x 376.4 cm (57.5 x 148.2 inches)

↓

Alice Bailly
Jeu d'éventail ou Femme à l'éventail
(Fan Game, or Woman with a Fan), 1913
Oil on canvas
92 x 73 cm (36.2 x 28.7 inches)

↓

Balthus (Balthazar Klossowski de Rola)
Le Roi des chats (The King of Cats), 1935
Oil on canvas
78 x 49.7 cm (30.7 x 19.5 inches)

→

Paul Klee
Am Nil (On the Nile), 1939
Distemper paint on paper mounted on jute
75 x 125 cm (29.5 x 49.2 inches)

Klee

Bonne Année

←

Aloïse Blanche Corbaz
Bonne année (recto) (*Happy New Year*)
4th period: 1951–60
Colored crayon on paper
52.8 x 84.1 cm (20.8 x 33.1 inches)

↓

Bruce Nauman
Untitled (Hand Circle), 1996
Bronze
12.7 x 67.3 x 63.5 cm (5 x 26.5 x 25 inches)

↑

Anselm Kiefer
Die Rheintöchter (The Rhine Daughters), 1982–2013
Collage of wood-block prints, acrylic and varnish on canvas
190 x 330 x 5.5 cm (74.8 x 129.9 x 2.1 inches)

ter
Woglinde
Floßhilde

↑
Philippe Decrauzat
Untitled, 2001
Acrylic on canvas
140 x 245 cm (55.1 x 96.4 inches)

Toward a New Cultural Hub

The Bellerive Site, a Competition and a Project

The Bellerive site chosen for the new museum is located near the Bellerive-Plage swimming pool and bathing area at the edge of the lake and belonged to the city of Lausanne. Not very far from the Olympic Museum and in an area set aside for leisure activities, the relatively open site was, on the other hand, at a certain distance from the city center.

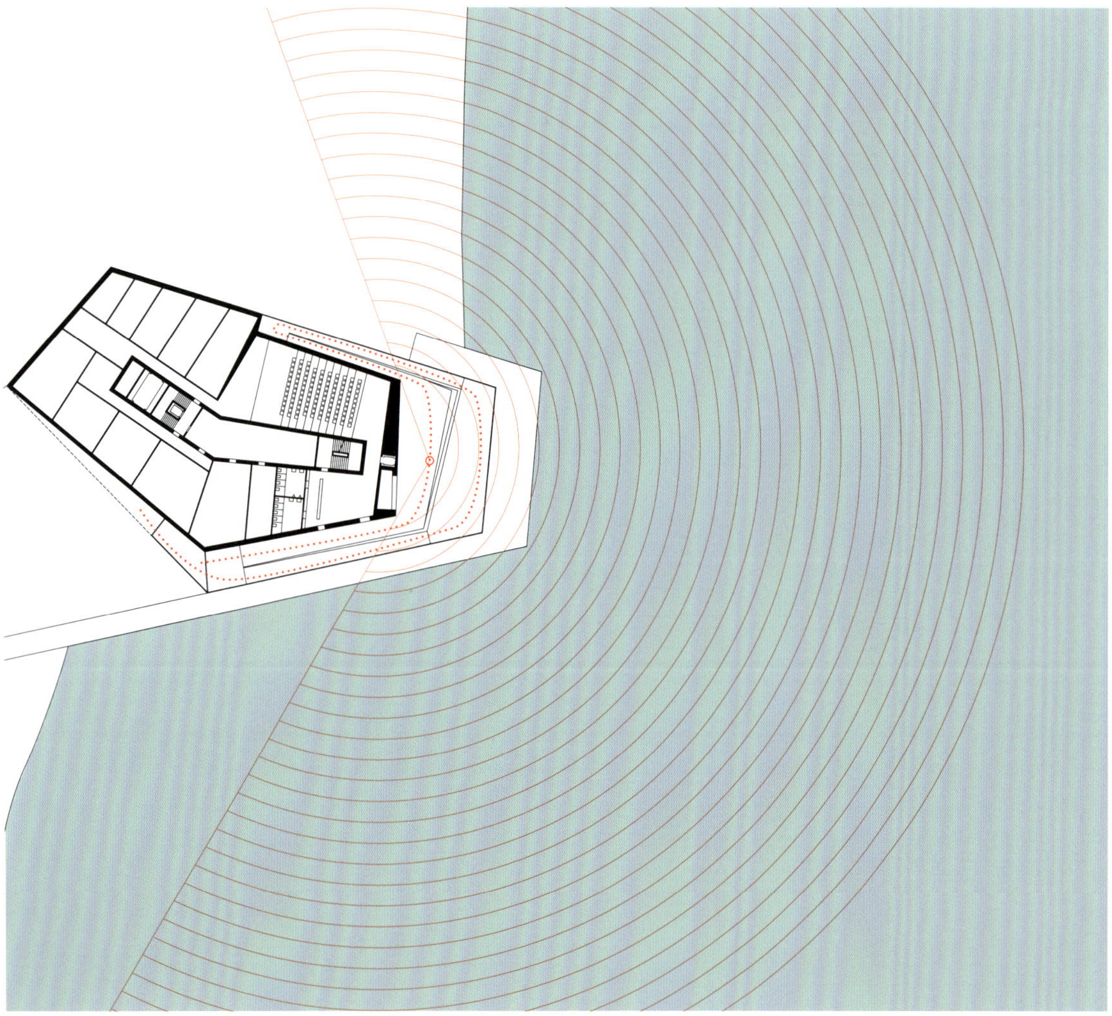

Ten minutes from the subway line running to the main train station and close to the port of the CGN passenger boats that navigate on the lake, Bellerive is also close to the UNIL (University of Lausanne) and EPFL (Federal Polytechnic of Lausanne) campuses, with unobstructed views of the lake and the Alps beyond. Finally, and perhaps not least of all, this area along the lake is historically the point of origin of Lausanne, where its first inhabitants lived thousands of years ago.

The competition documents limited the height of the future building to 12 meters in order not to block the sunlight of the neighboring pool but imposed few other restrictions. The lakeside location, on rubble left from the 1964 National Exhibition which was held on the site, above a fairly deep layer of sandy soil, implied some structural constraints, but the relatively steady levels of the lake did not imply special precautions against flooding.

In September 2003, the government reaffirmed the will to build a new museum on the Bellerive site, to be inaugurated in 2009. The two-step international architectural competition for the building was launched on February 20, 2004, with the goal of receiving proposals in July 2004, and then reducing the number of entries being considered to twelve for the second phase. The competition documents specified not only that the facilities for a modern museum had to be taken into account, but also that the constraints of the site and ecological concerns had to be part of any project. Presided by Philippe Biéler, a former Green party State Councilor (Conseiller d'Etat), the jury included the director of the Museum, Yves Aupetittallot, the Canton architect, Eric Perrette, and the architects Gonçalo Byrne (Portugal), Oriol Bohigas (Spain), Sandra Giraudi (Lugano), and Silvia Gmür (Basel). The program called for 1,800 square meters of permanent exhibition galleries, 1,200 square meters of temporary shows, 205 square meters of offices, and 800 square meters of reserves, as well as various public and technical spaces. One hundred parking spots were also part of the scheme.

In April 2004, it was announced that 250 dossiers had been received from architects located in thirteen European countries, with twelve selected for the second phase. This final group was given until December of that year to submit a more specific project, with the announcement of the winner scheduled for February 2005. Projects were submitted by such international architects and designers as Dominique Perrault (Paris), MVRDV (Rotterdam), Mario Bellini (Milan), François Roche (Paris), who submitted a project in collaboration with the artist Philippe Parreno, and NO.MAD (Madrid). Roche and NO.MAD were among the nine finalists, together with seven Swiss-based teams. These two teams, respectively placed sixth and seventh in the competition, proposed a more significant integration of the building(s) into a green environment than the other contestants.

The first prize project, called Ying Yang, was designed by Berrel Wülser Kräutler Architekten from Zurich. Their monolithic polygonal concrete form was set on a point jutting out toward the lake. Relatively blank, the project did allow for some windows facing the lake, using reflecting glass in the exhibition areas. Controversial from the first, the Ying Yang project, slated to cost CHF 68 million, was the object of a concerted campaign to halt the work. Led by Freddy Buache, the founder of the Swiss Film Archive (Cinémathèque), Michel Thévoz, former director of the Musée de l'Art Brut, and the well-known environmental activist Franz Weber, the campaign received enough signatures in 2008 to require a local ballot. Aside from aesthetic opposition to the project, opponents called for the new museum to be closer to the old city center, where the Place de la Riponne is located. The referendum held on November 30, 2008, resulted in a rejection of funding for the project. Subsequent to this vote, three members of the government of the Canton, Anne-Catherine Lyon, Pascal Broulis and François Marthaler, set in motion an effort to find a new location for the future museum.

↑

Bearel Wülser Kräutler Architekten
Computer-generated image of the competition-winning proposal for the Bellerive site next to the lake

All Aboard, Platform 10

Having examined eleven potential sites, including the Place de la Riponne in front of the Palais de Rumine, which was favored by the commission established to select the site, the Conseil d'Etat of Vaud announced on September 30, 2009, that a 25,000-square-meter lot next to the main railway station of Lausanne had been decided on.

Preference was given to the site near the station by the Etat de Vaud in part because the station and its vicinity is due to undergo a very considerable reconstruction that will certainly make this part of the city more attractive. The decision on the site, and the allotment of a CHF 13.87-million credit in June 2010, allowed for the organization of a new architectural competition for the Museum of Fine Arts, and also for an ideas competition related to two other buildings, to house the Musée de l'Elysée photography museum and the Musée de design et d'arts appliqués contemporains (mudac, Design and Contemporary Applied Arts Museum). The major innovation of the CFF railway site was, indeed, the fact that it would become a cultural hub with three museums as opposed to the single institution (Museum of Fine Arts) that was slated for the Bellerive site. The very fact that the photography and design museums could be grouped with the Museum of Fine Arts was due to the sheer size of the CFF site. The competition announcement brought proposals from 136 candidates from sixteen different countries. Eighteen architectural offices were invited to participate in the actual competition and the Barcelona-based team Estudio Barozzi Veiga was selected on June 9, 2011.

On October 5, 2011, the city of Lausanne acquired the site, formerly reserved to the locomotive sheds of the CFF Federal railway company in exchange for other parcels of land. As part of this procedure which involved giving the site to the Canton, five million Swiss francs were provided as a first sum for construction of the new museum. A formal land-use plan for the project (Plan d'affectation cantonal PAC) was proposed between August and September of 2012. Opposition to the scheme brought court challenges which were rejected by the court of the Canton and then by the Federal court, allowing the PAC to come into effect on October 8, 2014. On December 18, 2013, a further credit of CHF 30.6 million, accompanied by funds for studies of the future Elysée / mudac buildings and plans for the old Palais de Rumine, was proposed and formally adopted by the government of Vaud in March 2014.

The site of the new Museum of Fine Arts and future Elysée (photography) and mudac (design) museums is set directly next to the main railway station of Lausanne, on the site of the former locomotive maintenance sheds. This location is actually just 800 meters from the Palais de Rumine where the Museum was formerly housed. Despite the short distance involved, this transition also marks a basic shift away from the early twentieth-century city to a more modern configuration.

The Lausanne Railway Station

Subsequent to the opening of the Simplon Tunnel on May 19, 1906, an architectural competition was launched in 1908 for the design of a new central railway station for Lausanne. The competition was won by the architects Monod & Laverrière associated with Taillens & Dubois. The architect responsible for the project was Albert Weiss. The competition documents stipulated that the station should have a "functional appearance, a façade that is dignified but not ostentatious, using materials that are known to be unchanging, and if possible, locally quarried stone. The main entrance should have character, have harmonious proportions and be elegant without appearing to be too rich." The station was built between 1911 and 1916. A significant feature of the station is the metal and glass *marquise* that covers the tracks at a maximum height of 16.5 meters, a length of 107 meters, and a width of 44 meters. This part of the station was completed in March 1912. The design of this distinctive feature was the work of the engineers of the CFF, Adolphe Robert-Regarmey and Léon Marguerat-Blanc. A second *marquise* covers the number one track, located closest to the station itself. The opening of the Simplon Tunnel and the new railway station in Lausanne allowed the city to become a stop of the legendary Simplon-Orient Express, as of April 16, 1919, bringing tourists from Paris in one direction and from Eastern Europe in the other.

As was often the case in period structures, the Lausanne railway station includes a Buffet, opened in 1916, with panoramic paintings representing Neuchâtel, La Chaux-de-Fonds, Bern, Montreux, Fribourg, Zermatt, and Geneva. Closed in 2015, the Buffet was restored and reopened in 2018. As of 1984, regular high-speed TGV service between the Gare de Lyon in Paris and Lausanne was established, increasing the importance of the station as a regional hub. Recognized as a Swiss cultural landmark of national importance, the station was renovated between 1992 and 1996. By 2030, the Lausanne railway station is slated to undergo a 1.2-billion-franc transformation. The platforms will be extended to a length of 400 meters in order to receive longer trains with a higher passenger capacity. Retail spaces in the station will be increased from 2,500 square meters to 10,000 square meters.

The CFF Locomotive Sheds

The new cultural hub of Lausanne, and in particular the Museum of Fine Arts, was built on the site of the former locomotive maintenance sheds used by the CFF, the Swiss National Railways. The first locomotive sheds for the Lausanne station were built before the completion of the station in 1911 and a second section was added at the time of the 1964 National Exhibition. The 1911 building was nearly 133 meters long and consisted of two 41 × 43-meter rectangular blocks with eight tracks, each providing space for sixteen locomotives, which were usually serviced at night. The sheds had 35-meter-high brick chimneys and wooden roofs. It has been noted that shortly after the construction of the original locomotive sheds, it became common in Europe for such facilities to be located further away from the stations they serve. Thus, in a sense, the sheds bear witness to railway design that was common at the beginning of the twentieth century but changed not long thereafter. Because of its location near the entrance to the central station of Lausanne, but in an area reserved to the use of the railway company, these sheds were a relatively little-known element of the industrial heritage of the city, but were considered, because of their unusual, elongated design, ample presence of natural light and other factors, to be of interest. In 2009, the locomotive sheds were used by a workforce of forty persons who were still responsible for the upkeep of the locomotives of the CFF, but the facilities were no longer used after 2011. The locomotive sheds were demolished beginning on February 16, 2016. By May of the same year, only the central block with its characteristic curved window remained, destined to be integrated into the new Museum which was to be built on the site of the former locomotive sheds. It may be interesting to note that the very proximity of the site to active railway tracks had an influence on the design. On June 29, 1994, a freight train including three tank cars carrying potentially hazardous substances derailed in the station. Despite a high level of vigilance, the continued risk of incidents of this nature led to the requirement that the long southern façade of the Museum along the railway tracks be protected and have relatively little glazing.

Appeals against the project were rejected by the courts at the end of 2015, and the Federal court allowed the demolition of the buildings on the site to proceed. Work on the site of the new museum began in early 2016, with a formal laying of the first stone on October 6 of the same year.

D21
Véhicule de sauvetage
www.

SBB CFF FFS
D20
50

26b
27b
28b

New Competition, New Architects

The competition organized for the design of the new museum and for ideas concerning the broader site was announced on July 20, 2010. The jury was presided by Olivier Steimer, president of the Banque Cantonale Vaudoise, with the architect David Chipperfield as vice president. Other jury members were Daniel Brélaz (syndic or mayor of Lausanne), Bernard Fibicher (director of the Museum), Pierre Keller (director of the ECAL school of art and design), and the architects Patrick Devanthéry, Francisco Aires Mateus, and Charles Pictet, among others. The total site area under consideration was 21,000 square meters directly next to railway tracks on the southern side and an embankment with apartment buildings to the north. Logically one announced objective of the competition beyond the actual architecture was to seek a method to open this relatively circumscribed area to the rest of the city. In terms of visitors, the competition documents stressed that the new institution should be open to the local population, to tourists, and to school groups. The total public floor area of the Museum was fixed at 4,920 square meters with a further 3,170 square meters for the reserves, offices, and other administrative spaces. The concomitant ideas competition was focused on the future development of the entire site as a "cultural pole" for the city and the Canton, to include another significant structure housing the Musée de l'Elysée and the mudac, respectively dedicated to photography and to design. The architects involved in the competition were further invited to suggest ways to develop the activities of the site even beyond the planned buildings, with a further 1,000 square meters explicitly set aside for that purpose.

The jury met and considered 136 projects on October 7, 2010. Eighteen teams were selected for the second phase of the process. Among those selected were Harry Gugger (Basel), Nieto Sobejano (Madrid), Barozzi Veiga (Barcelona), Allied Works (New York), Kengo Kuma (Tokyo), Caruso St John (London), Bernard Tschumi (New York), and Eduardo Souto de Moura (Lisbon). By way of contrast, Zaha Hadid Architects in London sent a submission that was not retained for the second phase of the competition. One direct participant says that with the presence of David Chipperfield, the goal for the jury was to select an attractive and functional museum project, "and not just an architectural gesture." Together with a number of other Swiss and international teams, this selection was clearly at a very high international level. The jury met again to consider the final proposals of the architects in May 2011. One interesting comment of the jury on the eighteen proposals was that "in examining the projects, it became clear that the objectives of the client at times appeared to be antithetical and could thus not all be satisfied. Indeed, a good number of the architects concerned hesitated between the will to preserve the historic substance of the railway site, that of creating an institution with a strong presence in an animated part of the city, and the insertion of a cultural district within a perimeter that was partially and intentionally left up to the competitors." On May 23, 2011, the Italian-Spanish team Barozzi Veiga was selected. The runners up were respectively Caruso St John and MADE IN SÀRL (Lausanne). It is interesting to note that two of these three teams—Barozzi Veiga and MADE IN SÀRL—were selected by the jury "au titre de la relève," meaning that they were younger and perhaps less established than many of the other competing firms. Barozzi Veiga took it upon themselves to essentially suggest the demolition of the locomotive sheds on the site, while conserving outlines of the forms of the older building on the southern (railway track) side of the building and on the eastern façade as well. Caruso St John made a much more literal use of the existing buildings.

The Barozzi Veiga Approach

Fabrizio Barozzi, born in 1976 in Rovereto, Italy, studied architecture at the Istituto Universitario di Architettura in Venice and went on to the Escuela Técnica Superior de Arquitectura de Sevilla and from there to the Ecole d'Architecture de Paris La Villette. Beginning in 2007, he was a Professor at the International University of Catalonia in Barcelona and after 2009, at the University of Girona. From 2016–18 he was a Visiting Professor at the Massachusetts Institute of Technology (MIT). Alberto Veiga was born in 1973 in Santiago de Compostela, Spain, and studied architecture at the Escuela Técnica Superior de Arquitectura de Navarra. Between 2007 and 2010 he was a Professor at the International University of Catalonia in Barcelona and in 2014 he was a Visiting Professor at the Istituto Universitario di Architettura in Venice. Barozzi Veiga was founded in Barcelona by Fabrizio Barozzi and Alberto Veiga in 2004. The pair has worked on both public and private projects and received a number of awards, including the prestigious Mies van der Rohe Award for European Architecture (2015, Szczecin Philharmonic Hall), the RIBA Award for International Excellence (2018, Bündner Kunstmuseum Chur), and were candidates for the 2017–18 Swiss Architectural Award.

One of the most significant works by Barozzi Veiga is the Szczecin Philharmonic Hall in Poland. The design was influenced by the urban surroundings and, in particular, by the "verticality of the city's residential buildings, by the monumentality of the upright ornaments of its neo-Gothic churches and the heavy volumes of its Classicist buildings, by the towers that dot its entire skyline and the cranes of its port," according to the architects. The Philharmonic Hall was the first structure in Poland to win the prestigious Mies van der Rohe Award, which is given every two years to a European building. Experts and European institutions nominate recently completed buildings for the Award with an overall list in 2015 of 420 buildings. Barozzi Veiga was chosen in particular because of their attention to context, a significant factor in the jury's consideration. Fabrizio Barozzi states: "We try to work with the uniqueness of each place, to avoid generic architecture and to avoid being self-referential. It was important for us to learn from the context and try to transform it. We want to support a new vision."

→

Fabrizio Barozzi and Alberto Veiga
photographed in their office in Barcelona

↓

Szczecin Philharmonic Hall
by Barozzi Veiga (Poland, 2014),
winner of the 2015 Mies van der Rohe Award
for European Architecture

↓

Bündner Kunstmuseum Chur extension
by Barozzi Veiga
[Switzerland, 2012–16]

The building was designed for a 1000-seat symphony hall, a 200-seat auditorium for chamber music, a multifunctional space for exhibitions and conferences, and a generous foyer. A single path through the building connects the different functions. The project had a considerable local importance because the new building occupied the site of the historic Konzerthaus which was destroyed during World War II. A double-skin façade provides acoustic insulation and natural ventilation. A LED system was employed to allow the building to appear to glow while using little electricity. The design of the main concert hall references more traditional spaces through the use of gold leaf but is based on the use of a mathematical sequence, with the fragmentation of the design increasing with its distance from the stage.

Previous winners of the Award have included such prestigious figures as Alvaro Siza (1988), Norman Foster (1990), Peter Zumthor (1998), Rem Koolhaas (2005), and David Chipperfield (2011). Indeed, the full list of winners since its creation in 1988 reads like a Who's Who of contemporary architecture, certainly a propitious indication for the future of Barozzi Veiga. The jury statement reads in part: "The series of pitched gables which crowns the rectangular complex of the new building dialogues well with the silhouette of the nearby Castle. The main symphony hall is clad in triangular wooden acoustic panels gilded with gold leaf. A large hall with the cafeteria and two grand open stairs take the role of a new covered square in the cold seasons, while multifunctional rooms wrap around the concert halls, offering new chances for cultural and leisure events. This winning project finds a convincing formal and spatial strategy for a city which strives for a better future in a fast-changing economy and social patterns, delivering a dignity to urban life and at the same time enhancing the city's specific historical identity with a contemporary 'monument'."

Alberto Veiga has stated: "We always look at the city first. It is more important than our building. Simply focusing on whether one likes the surroundings of the building or not is the wrong approach. There is no point simply paying attention to which building you dislike, or which structure is more beautiful than your own design. To take the museum in Chur as an example, the Villa Planta and the other surrounding buildings are part of our family. We have to live with them and share the city with them. Our building is part of the city. Our aim is therefore to rediscover the city, and to develop good answers that harmonize as well as possible with the surrounding conditions and circumstances. The best advice for an architect confronted with a complex environment is to respect the city, and to improve it if at all possible. That is the challenge." It is certainly to be noted that the outlines, indeed the forms, of the Szczecin Philharmonic Hall surely evoke the city as it exists, but as is evident in aerial views, the whiteness of the building stands in contrast to the urban environment. The Mies van der Rohe jury refers to a "contemporary monument" and that is precisely what the architects have created in Poland, a synthesis of integration into a historic context and the development of a modern form.

The Bündner Kunstmuseum Chur had been housed exclusively in the Villa Planta, a private residence built between 1874 and 1875 as a home for Jacques Ambrosius von Planta by the local architect Johannes Ludwig. The façade of this square Neoclassical building has a portico with supporting columns and steps that are flanked by sculptures of sphinxes. A golden dome topped by a half-moon evoke the owner's commercial ties to Egypt. Dedicated to artists from Switzerland's Graubünden region, the museum has a collection of 8,000 works dating from the eighteenth century to the present. It includes works by Angelika Kauffmann (1741–1807), the Giacometti family (Giovanni, Augusto, and Alberto), Ernst Ludwig Kirchner (1880–1938), and Not Vital (born in 1948). A 1990 renovation of the original building was carried out by Peter Zumthor, Peter Calonder, and Hans-Jörg Ruch.

The 4,000-square-meter extension for the museum designed by Barozzi Veiga (2012–16), after they won an international competition, takes the unusual approach of situating the exhibition spaces below grade, reducing its footprint and allowing an existing garden to be extended near the entrance. They explain: "The project absorbs and transforms the Palladian order and the Orientalist style, the main compositional features of the Villa Planta, through a central and symmetric composition scheme which gives the extension a clear formal autonomy as well as allowing the proposal to preserve the identity of the villa itself. The new addition to the Bündner Kunstmuseum is conceived as a simple and compact volume that becomes perfectly integrated into its immediate surroundings. The clarity with which it states its independence with respect to the adjacent buildings also reinforces the importance given to the garden that appears in the newly extended area and confers a sober presence to the building." The architects further explain that "the process of the purging of superfluous elements which began with the designs for Piloña and Lausanne reaches a point of maturity in the Bündner Museum." Barozzi Veiga was awarded third prize in a 2010 competition to design the new Neanderthal Museum in Piloña, which they said was "like a fossil embedded in the valley," a "seemingly primitive edifice." Indeed, the "reduced and minimalist" nature of the Piloña proposal and the realization in Chur do bear striking similarities to the Lausanne museum—at least in terms of a kind of geometric austerity

↓

Museum of Maritime History
rendering by Barozzi Veiga
(Saint-Malo, France, 2017)

↓

Neanderthal Museum
rendering by Barozzi Veiga
(Piloña, Spain, 2010)

and the attention to the pronounced texture of the structures. The Chur building uses an ordered pattern of 4,600 50-centimeter-square, molded-concrete textile blocks for its façades. The commentary of RIBA in connection with the 2018 Award for International Excellence reads in part: "The brief sought to extend the gallery by three times the existing floor area—the architects won the competitionby placing a modest cubic block behind the existing villa and building new gallery spaces across the entire plot—below ground. The elemental cubic block certainly sits well adjoining the villa and there is reciprocity in form—the architect quoted Piero della Francesca's double portrait, saying that independently each portrait would not make sense, only as a diptych does it work… Overall this is a very accomplished work, an elegant, minimal edifice in the city."

Contemporary architecture for the most part long ago abandoned the ideas of Gropius and others who favored the *tabula rasa*, which is to say a negation of the past. Nor has the superficial pastiche that appeared with such insistence in the 1970s under the "Postmodern" label endured. Rather it would seem in a very real and deep sense that the search at the heart of contemporary architecture, particularly the history-laden environment of Europe, is for a real link between past and present. Not a superficial one of appearance but something closer to the heart of form and space. In this respect, the historical and urban context of a project as significant as the Museum of Fine Arts in Lausanne becomes an essential element of any design. It may be, though, that these references are sublimated in some instances to the point of not being readily apparent. Barozzi and Veiga have taken a strong and perhaps brave approach in generating projects that approach minimalism. They have something of the stripped-down spirit of David Chipperfield and yet they also dare to use rougher materials, textured concrete, or vast surfaces in gray brick, as is the case in Lausanne. Their selection for the Mies van der Rohe Award was neither an accident nor a "one-off" event; it was, instead, the reflection of a real, emerging talent. Liking their work may not always be easy. There appears to be a massive and somewhat blank appearance in some of their projects that carries a weight that might be considered ominous for some. Though anecdotal, the use of one of their images in a recent movie is indicative of the mood their work strikes, but also of the fact that their work has already penetrated numerous cultural layers, from the top down. A space seen in the movie *Blade Runner 2049* (Dennis Villeneuve, 2017), presented as the office of the film's antagonist, is, in fact, derived from a Barozzi Veiga drawing of the unbuilt museum in Piloña. The film is dark and worrisome (described as "neo-noir science fiction"). The idea of the "weight" of the architecture of Barozzi Veiga bears some reflection. Theirs are very real, tangible buildings, where the evanescence of some contemporary architecture attempts to obviate solidity. Light is present, often streaming in from above, as it does in the Piloña drawing. Below, in the realm of the real users of the buildings, there is a sense of ordered calm and intelligence that is the hallmark of architects who have gone beyond trying to please in any superficial way. Their structures are substantial, even as they find a place in dense urban environments, or next to historic buildings. Just as they developed the unexpected solution of placing galleries below grade in Chur, leaving only a solid, textured cube as an entrance, they show an absence of dogmatism, a natural sense of correct architectural solutions and, still, a will to generate powerful forms that are very much of our time. These forms resonate with their environment even when their modernity is evident, a sure sign that Barozzi and Veiga are on to something.

Monolithic Modern — Comparable New Museum Buildings

Three museums in Europe of varying scale, recently enlarged or renovated, offer a comparison to the Museum of Fine Arts, Lausanne in terms of architectural design. Two of them, the Tate Modern Blavatnik Building and the Kunstmuseum Basel Extension rely, like the Lausanne building, on an extensive use of bricks for their façades. All three propose very contemporary, apparently blank façades.

Tate Modern, Blavatnik Building, London, UK, 2016

Tate Modern (1998–2000) marked the emergence of Herzog & de Meuron on the international scene and became the most visited museum of modern art in the world. Carefully studying the needs of the museum and of the neighborhood, the architects embarked on a requested expansion of the original facility, called the Tate Modern Project. They settled on an eleven-level, 64.5-meter-high, twisting, pyramidal form. Subterranean oil tanks earlier restored by the same team (2012) to create extra exhibition space lie below the new edifice. Doubling the gallery space of Tate Modern, the new building also creates a number of public spaces. A new museum entrance has been added on the southern side, as well as a north-south passage leading from the Thames to a new city plaza on Sumner Street. Concerning the main façade material, the architects state: “We wanted the combined elements of Tate Modern, old and new, to be expressed as a whole, to have them come together and function as a single organism. Using the same base palette of bricks and brickwork in a radical new way, we created a perforated brick screen through which light filters in the day and through which the building will glow at night.” Originally called the Switch House, because its construction required the displacement of part of the central electricity infrastructure of the old power plant, and now the Blavatnik Building, the structure was completed in 2016. Its floor area is 23,600 square meters and it was built in brick, concrete, steel, and oak for a cost of £260 million. By way of comparison, the new Lausanne Museum of Fine Arts has a floor area of 8,090 square meters. The two clearly share an extensive use of brick and an origin that is related to industrial infrastructure.

Kunstmuseum Basel Extension, Basel, Switzerland, 2016

Located directly across the street from the existing building of the Kunstmuseum Basel, in the heart of the city, this extension is connected to the earlier structure via a generous tunnel. Of equal height, the two buildings respond to each other in subtle ways, underlined by the unusual gray-brick façade chosen by the Basel architects Christ & Gantenbein. Each floor of the new building has two exhibition galleries connected vertically by a monumental central staircase topped by a large round skylight. An unexpected, uniform lighting system that relies in good part on neon lights, plays against the rather monumental density of the structure. The materials employed include the façades in water-struck bricks (Petersen Tegl), and inside, galvanized steel, Bardiglio marble, scraped plaster, oak parquet, and prefabricated concrete beams. An unusual feature of the building is an external computer-controlled LED system that allows the museum to write the name of the current exhibition on the façade using no more than light. The floor area of the extension is 4,426 square meters.

Museum of Arts, Nantes, France, 2017

Designed by the London architects Stanton Williams selected in a 2009 competition, this project involved the renovation of an existing nineteenth-century museum and the addition of 4,000 square meters of contemporary art exhibition space on four levels. The Musée d'arts de Nantes is, along with Rouen, Lille, Lyon, Grenoble, and Montpellier, one of the largest "provincial" museums in France. The total floor area of the project was 17,000 square meters and the construction budget was 48.8 million euros, paid for by the city and the region Nantes Métropole. An auditorium, library, new educational facilities, archive, and external sculpture court were also created. A landscape design connects to the museum from the surrounding Place de Oratoire and Botanical Gardens, emphasizing the museum's central role in the urban fabric of the area. A consistent palette of materials was applied in the renovated spaces, giving the impression that the museum is a monolithic volume, "carved out of a single block of stone." Translucent laminated marble was used to cover the south elevation of the new extension. The lead architect at Stanton Williams in charge of the project, Patrick Richard, stated: "The new Museum has been conceived around the existing collections, creating an intimate dialog between art and architecture that firmly embeds the new Museum within the distinctive historical setting of the city."

Architecture and Art

From Construction to Completion

Several top architectural photographers covered the project from construction to completion. The portfolio on the following pages was realized by Jesus Arenas, Yves André, Matthieu Gafsou, and Simon Menges at the request of the architects and of the client.

26b
27b
28b

D21

41
CONRAD KERN

We try to work with the uniqueness of each place, to avoid generic architecture and to avoid being self-referential. It was important for us to learn from the context and try to transform it. We want to support a new vision.

Fabrizio Barozzi

PARKING MONTBENON

Lausanne

www.sbb.ch

SBB CFF FFS
www.cff.ch

We find that the stairway is a public element—it is a kind of huge bench. The location of the entrance was determined by the existing remnant of the south façade and the large semi-circular window. The idea was to reuse the window from the old locomotive shed which is located here not only as a symbolic or formal element. We also wanted visitors to be able to have a direct view of the trains and the tracks. We wanted to show them that the soul of this part of the city is visible in the train tracks. People can go up the stairs and discover the context, and then they can decide on their pathway into the galleries.

Alberto Veiga

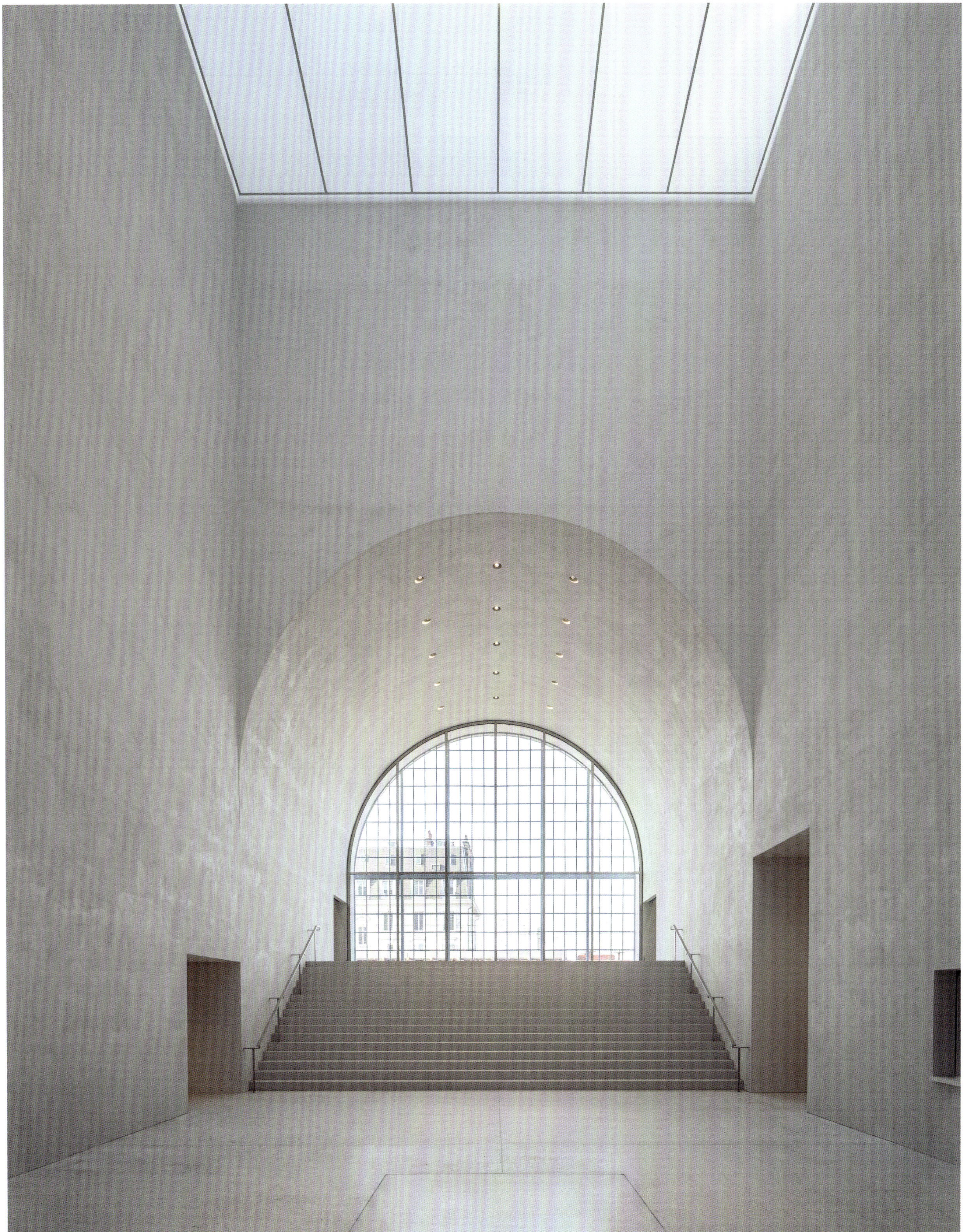

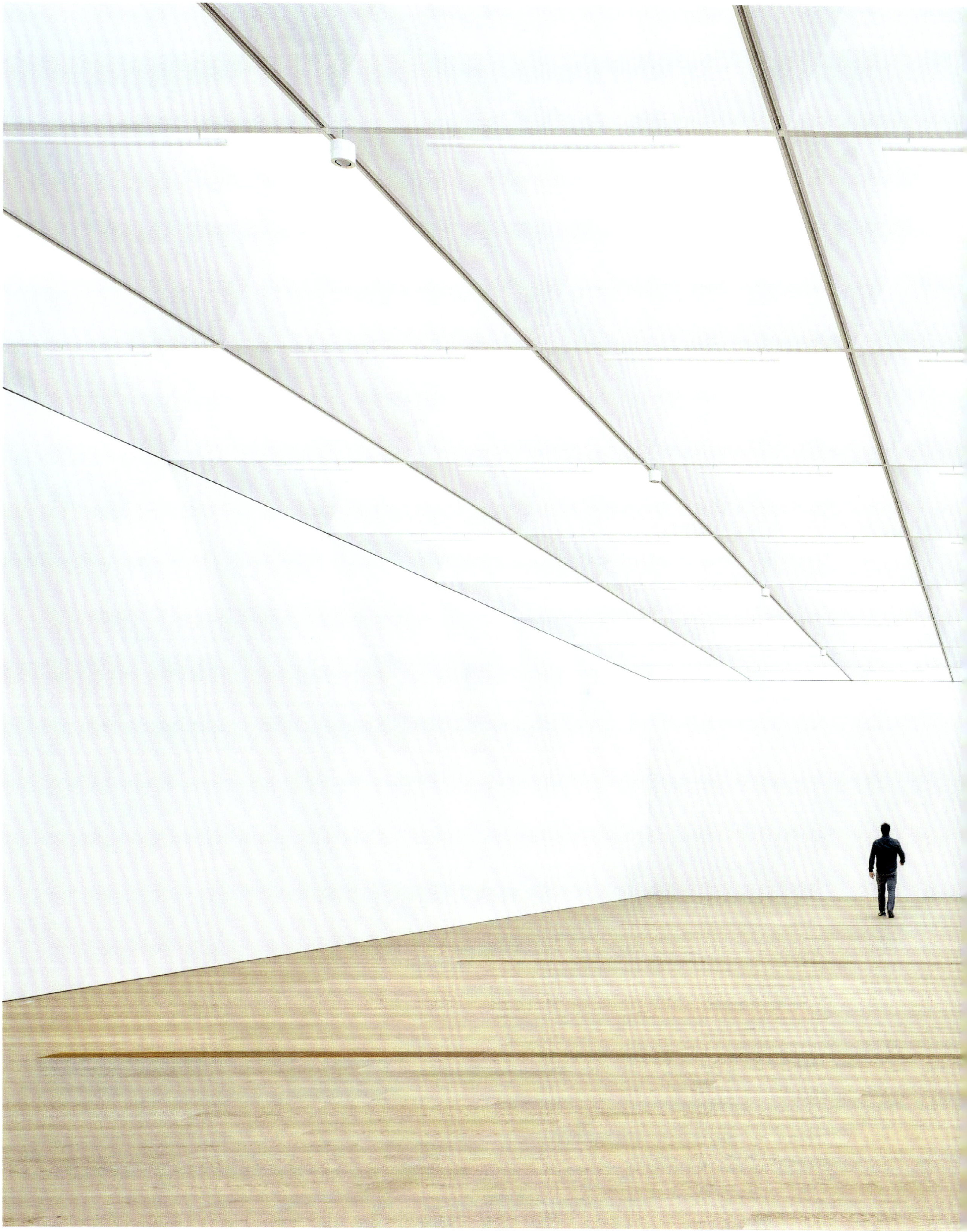

SBB CFF FFS

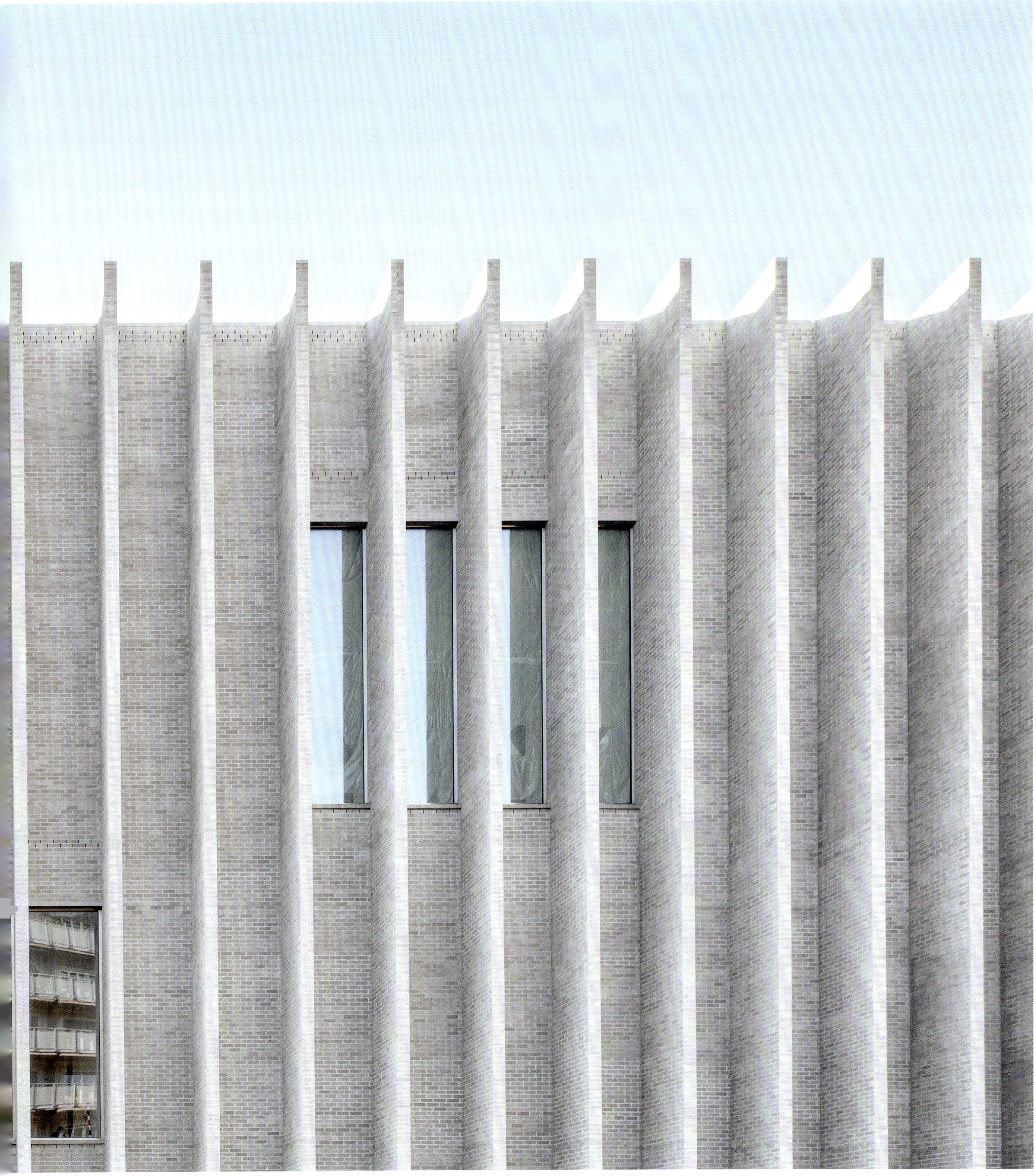

A New Home for Art

↑

Sketch by Fabrizio Barozzi
for the Museum of Fine Arts, Lausanne

In the Words of the Architects

Alberto Veiga and his partner Fabrizio Barozzi are the architects of the new Museum of Fine Arts, Lausanne. Although the team did build another museum project in Switzerland (Chur) in between, the Lausanne project was their first and largest museum. Alberto Veiga responds here to questions from the author during a visit of the new building in February 2019.

Philip Jodidio: How did you decide where to place the building in the overall site?

Alberto Veiga: The pathway between the old locomotive sheds and the existing stone arcade was only four to five meters wide, so the north façade of the new Museum is quite a bit further back in the direction of the current railway tracks. The original sheds were much wider. The competition suggested that the old building should be preserved, but we did not know how to do that. A key point in our design was when we forgot about the old building and started to think about the public space. We decided to create a public square with a background of three simple pieces. At the time, the Elysée and mudac museums were meant to be housed in separate structures. Our goal was not to echo earlier buildings on the site, but to compose the best public space that we could achieve. The place of the building, its materiality, and its rhythm are, of course, influenced by the railway tracks. Our scheme had to do with the mood and the atmosphere that we felt in this place.

PJ: The building is quite strict in plan and elevation—it is a large rectangular block with the only extrusion being on the south side where the large window of the former locomotive sheds was preserved. Why is that?

AV: The geometry is clearly linked to our approach to architecture. We like to be expressive but with simple gestures. We are trying to find what I would call *essentiality* in our proposal. We are not minimalists. We try to be expressive. The shape of the Museum is quite simple and in fact it is a kind of barrier or wall that protects the public space from the trains. It protects the public from the noise and presence of the tracks. The public space we created is also for the neighborhood to the north and the Museum building thus stands apart from the apartment buildings above. The Museum is a kind of background for the neighbors and for the public space, and that is why it appears to be so simple in its basic form.

PJ: How did you seek to contextualize the project, to derive something from its precise location?

AV: The Museum does seek to incorporate elements of the context. The rhythm of the pilasters is derived from the rhythm of the tracks and the railroad ties.

In this kind of industrial area, repeated rhythms are found frequently, and we wanted to keep that in our project somehow. The pilasters allow us to introduce windows or doors in a determined pattern. When you walk through the public space from the entrance area near the railway station, you start to perceive the windows and the life inside the building. There is a concept of contrasts—what you see from the entrance and what you discover when you walk by the building is something we wished to achieve from the beginning of the design. There is also the contrast in the perception of the building in the day and at night. The willful use of perception and contrast is a key to understanding what we sought to do. You perceive the building from a distance as a solid volume that changes and becomes less opaque when you pass by, or put on the lights inside; that is very important to us.

PJ: Why did you select gray bricks as the main cladding material?

AV: There is something around the site, in the city, that elicited the choice of gray bricks. When you see the completed building and the neighborhood, I think that it is a color that works. We wanted to give the impression that the bricks are handmade. These are clinker bricks, which are denser, heavier, and more irregular than standard bricks. From the outset we wanted to do something that would have a handmade aspect or appear to be the work of craftsmen. That somehow matched our concept of the building.

PJ: Would you prefer to compare the use of bricks to earlier industrial architecture, or, for example, to another cultural institution such as Peter Zumthor's Kolumba Museum (Cologne, 2007)?

AV: I don't think the building has an industrial appearance even if there are some elements, such as the pilasters, that find their origin in an echo of industry. I find that the reference to the Kolumba Museum by Peter Zumthor in terms of materiality is a good one. There is a shared understanding of how a museum today is to be made, with what kind of materials.

PJ: The eastern façade of the building, which faces the railway station, is the first image that visitors receive of the Museum. What is the concept of this design?

AV: When you come out of the train station and you discover the volume represented by the eastern façade, there is a play on perception and scale. When you see it from a distance, it is hard to determine if it is big or not. Playing on scale in that way was important for us. The façade itself does not really give a clue to its scale. That is something you discover progressively as you approach the building and walk past it.

In our original scheme we attached the surface of the eastern façade of the former locomotive sheds to the new brick wall. We decided, though, that we might not need the doors, or a reproduction of them. We were concerned that these remnants would be perceived as something too ornamental, or "fake." The former tracks have been preserved in front of the Museum entrance to the north and the extruded volume to the south, corresponding to the former locomotive sheds, is still there. Kenneth Frampton, who came to see us in Barcelona, disagreed with leaving any remnants of the old sheds. Our feeling is that the southern volume activates the conversation between the site, its history, the new building, and the visitors. At the request of the client, we did work on a form in metal mesh for the eastern façade that will evoke the memory of the old building.

PJ: Once past the eastern façade, visitors enter the public space on the northern side of the Museum, and find that the building is not as opaque as they might have expected, is that right?

AV: At the ground level on the north side, we have numerous windows that allow views into the public spaces, and out of course from the interior. The idea is to compose a kind of cultural street. The bookshop, the café, and the auditorium have windows that open to this esplanade. This was one of the very basic concepts of the project. Our goal as architects is to attract visitors who will experience the buildings, to suggest that something of interest is going on here. If the building is too obvious, you discover it once and then you don't come back.

PJ: On the southern side, the Museum is very close to the railway tracks.

AV: The trains are part of the essence of this building. What makes this project special is the fact that it is so close to the tracks and the trains. It is connected to the soul of the city, and to put the Museum of Fine Arts so close to the station is amazing.

PJ: The entrance door of the Museum is located in the center of the northern façade. That door seems quite small as compared to the very long structure. Why is that?

AV: It signifies a change of scale. Somehow it makes the attitude of the visitor change. You don't rush as much and maybe you speak more quietly when you enter through this type of doorway.

PJ: Inside, visitors discover a rather monumental staircase and a large semicircular window. What is the significance for you of these elements?

AV: We find that the stairway is a public element—it is a kind of huge bench.

The location of the entrance was determined by the existing remnant of the south façade and the large semicircular window. The idea was to reuse the window from the old locomotive shed which is located here not only as a symbolic or formal element. We also wanted visitors to be able to have a direct view of the trains and the tracks. We wanted to show them that the soul of this part of the city is visible in the train tracks. People can go up the stairs and discover the context, and then they can decide on their pathway into the galleries. The idea of framing the view in the entrance gives specificity to this space. We did not want to propose something generic—the specific nature of the site is visible.

PJ: The director of the Museum points out that the entrance or lobby is the only vertical element in an otherwise horizontal composition and that it naturally divides the functions of the Museum. Do you agree with that statement?

AV: We did not divide the building at the outset thinking of which functions would be on the right and which would be on the left, temporary and permanent exhibitions for example. We divided the building into two upper floors, one for permanent exhibitions and one for the temporary shows. The upper floor with the natural overhead lighting would have been for the temporary exhibitions. We felt that two staircases would allow the user to understand readily how to use the building. It was decided by the Museum that the entire first floor would not be devoted to permanent exhibitions. I believe that the design allows the Museum to organize its galleries any way it wants to. The ground floor is used for the main public spaces, the café, bookshop, auditorium, and the *Espace projets*, which is a kind of space for younger artists or freer interventions that is open in a direct way to the esplanade through large windows.

PJ: The building basically has only two windows that look out to the railway tracks with the lake visible in the distance only from one window. Why is that?

AV: We couldn't open any of the galleries on the south side because of risks to the works of art in terms of potential danger coming from the train tracks. That is why we have only two public windows facing south—at the top of the steps in the foyer, which existed in the earlier locomotive sheds, and a smaller one on the second-floor level of the other public stairway. That way, when people arrive at the top floor, they do have the view of the lake. I do believe that we would have had more windows on the south were it not for the programmatic requirement to plan for railway-side risks. Somehow, I do not miss seeing the lake more, but having more than one possible viewpoint was difficult for the reasons I have explained.

PJ: You of course worked with the director of the Museum and his team on the gallery design. Was anyone else involved in that process?

AV: We worked with the museum planner, Dieter Bogner, from the outset of the competition. This was our first experience working with a museum program. He gave us numerous ideas about how the galleries should be composed. He gave us advice about things to avoid but left us entirely free to do as we wished. The proportions of the galleries were worked out with the advice of Dieter Bogner and decided on by Bernard Fibicher. We discussed height and proportions and how many galleries would have artificial light and how many would have natural light from above. The gallery heights were stipulated in the competition brief, but the second-floor spaces were made higher (5.5 meters) in the process of the discussions. All the spaces were conceived so that they can readily be divided into at least two, and more for the upper galleries. Such elements as smoke detectors and the security installations have to be placed to take this kind of eventuality into account.

PJ: You have left small gaps between the walls and the floors in the galleries. Why is that?

AV: There is a change of materials between the floors and the white walls. Materials need to have some air around them. The wall seems to float above the floor. The Museum will be using temporary walls for hangings or exhibitions, and that joint or gap will also exist with the temporary walls. Even though the galleries will be divided, there will be continuity in the treatment of the surfaces.

PJ: You have also designed the furniture of the Museum.

AV: There are benches that we designed made of terrazzo and leather on the first floor and oak and steel details on the second floor. We designed all of the furniture, including the bookshop and restaurant.

PJ: The public spaces of the Museum and the galleries seem to be quite restrained in their expression, is that your intention?

AV: Our intention was to not overdesign the gallery spaces so that the architecture would not compete with the art. That was the main challenge for us. I think that you need to put the emphasis on the eyes and the feelings of the visitors, that is the most important point. Visitors need to feel as comfortable as possible in order to enjoy the artworks. Creating the conditions for that is our task as architects.

PJ: The proportions of interior spaces are also important in the design.

AV: The Museum is not huge, but the proportion of gallery spaces to circulation and other public areas is very good I think. There is also a question of a balance to be attained with the city—it is a very good size for Lausanne. I feel that the city has found a good balance between their expectations and the reality of the city.

PJ: Some say that this Museum is well suited in its relative austerity and exterior grayness to the nature of this region, and perhaps to its Protestant background. Is that an idea that you accept?

AV: I like the comment, but we did not have that in mind. For the competition we were thinking about our architecture and the proposal. If people can identify with this kind of austerity and find a relation to the character of the people of this region, it sounds very good to me.

PJ: The word "austerity" does not bother you?

AV: No, I quite like it. I am not sure I always find the building austere however. I find that the clinker brick reacts quite well with the light. Rather than austerity, I feel that there is a kind of ambiguity about the building as you approach it. That is intentional and is why we restrained the overall geometry. We did not reduce the material palette to save money or to give the image that the building is not luxurious, no. We thought that the material choice would allow us to express simplicity. Using the same tonalities and textures results in a building becoming a kind of background for the city. The iconic element is the space in front of the building and not the building itself.

PJ: Emmanuel Ventura, the architect of the Canton, calls this the anti-Bilbao. Do you agree with that idea?

AV: In this site it would be very difficult to compete with the trains or even with the neighboring apartment buildings. We felt that trying to react with a more complex shape would have been the wrong approach. We decided what to do when we understood that the building is in fact a secondary actor of this intervention. The main actor is the square, the open public space. Everything is a result of that realization—the proportions, the materials, how the building fits into the site, and how future buildings would interact with our design to generate a new urban space. The main message of this project is that the architect has to look to the city and find references there. Here our fundamental goal is to create a public space. For us the real measure of success would be if the public square could be used as much as possible. That would mean that the building has somehow succeeded.

↓

In the entrance hall of the Museum
Giuseppe Penone
Luce e ombra (Light and Shadow), 2011
Bronze, gold leaf, and granite
1,450 x 470 x 490 cm (570.9 x 185 x 192.9 inches)

In the Words of the Director

Born in Sion (Valais) in 1957, Bernard Fibicher studied French and American literature and art history at the Universities of Zurich and Bern, obtaining a doctorate in the history of art. He worked as a curator in the Museum of Fine Arts in Sion (1982–95) before transferring to the Kunsthaus in Zurich and going from there to become the director of the Kunsthalle in Bern for seven years. He briefly directed the contemporary art project of the Bern Museum of Fine Arts (2005–06). He became the director of the Museum of Fine Arts, Lausanne in 2007, a position that he will retain until 2022. He responds here to questions from the author in February 2019.

Philip Jodidio: Are there some underlying currents in the exhibitions that you have organized, both in the more distant past and since becoming director of the Museum of Fine Arts, Lausanne in 2007?

Bernard Fibicher: In my previous positions and then in Lausanne, I presented exhibitions with artists from Africa, India, China and other countries. I organized the first European solo exhibition of Ai Wei Wei at the Bern Kunsthalle in 2004. An exhibition in Lausanne that I am particularly fond of was dedicated to the work of one of the important Indian artists, Nalini Malani (2010). That show demonstrated the openness of the Museum to creativity from other continents. Other Swiss museums tend to focus on Europe and the United States so showing artists like Nalini Malani and Ai Wei Wei has been a way to distinguish the Museum of Fine Arts, Lausanne from other institutions in the country. Our show on Russian landscapes in 2014 was one of the most successful in terms of attendance in the past twenty years. The Ai Wei Wei exhibition (2017–18), which was the last one in our old building, attracted more than 100,000 visitors. As is the case elsewhere, the public is attracted to well-known artists, but some themes that might seem exotic here, such as Russian landscapes, also met with public approval. The best known of these Russian artists was perhaps Ivan Chichkine (1832–98) and it is a safe bet that not many of our visitors knew that name. Clearly, people did not come to see the work of Chichkine, but because nineteenth-century Russian landscapes made them dream of something else than what they already know.

PJ: How does this experience inform your plans for exhibitions in the new building?

BF: We are what I would call generalists in terms of museum activity. The collections run from the eighteenth century to the present. Our temporary exhibitions will, of course, often have a connection to our own collections. The period around 1900 is one of our stronger points, with artists like Steinlen and Vallotton, and the Art Nouveau with Eugène Grasset. These artists often had a strong tie to Paris.

There was a constant back-and-forth at the time and many Swiss artists became partially French. Born in Lausanne in 1865, Vallotton became a French citizen in 1900. These relations have been extensively explored in our past exhibitions, so with the opening of the new Museum we will look in a different direction, to the east and Vienna. The first major temporary exhibition, *À fleur de peau. Vienna 1900, from Klimt to Schiele and Kokoschka*, will be held beginning on February 14, 2020. We will focus not only on painting but also on architecture and design, with seminal figures such as Adolf Loos and Josef Hoffmann. The Museum of Fine Arts, Lausanne is an institution of the Canton of Vaud, and we naturally have a mission to bring forward local talents. We will have a biennial exhibition in the summer under the title *Jardin d'Hiver*; the first edition will be held from June 19 to September 13, 2020. A guest curator will organize the event around a specific theme and invite artists from the region. We also have a strong interest in contemporary art and the first major show in that area will be on the work of Kiki Smith. Born in Germany in 1954, she is the daughter of the sculptor Tony Smith, and had a major retrospective of her work at the Walker Art Center in Minneapolis, the Whitney Museum in New York, and other American institutions in 2005. Her work has not been presented in Switzerland since a show at the Centre d'Art Contemporain (Geneva, 1990).

PJ: Are your exhibition plans directly related to the desire to bring in as many visitors as possible?

BF: Attendance figures are a motivation for any museum curator. We don't work in the hope that nobody will come to see an exhibition. I would say that we hope to draw the highest possible number of visitors that can be expected for a given subject. We have a rough idea of how many people will come, but there is a kind of arithmetic approach over a longer period. I would say my most important criterion is to assure that our program is respected by the art world. The second most important factor is to see if our shows truly interest the public. We do not create an exhibition because we want to have, say, 100,000 visitors in a three-month period, but, if it happens, we are of course pleased. Our inaugural hanging is focused on donations to the Museum, and in particular recent ones. This is our way of thanking those who have made donations of works, or of collections of art.

PJ: Will your relation to the public change in a fundamental way with the opening of the new building?

BF: At the outset, of course, people come with two objectives in mind. They want to discover the new building, to look at its architecture, and to admire or criticize it. A few months later we will present our first large-scale temporary exhibition on Vienna in 1900, and that will be an occasion for visitors to return, less for the architecture and more for the art. We are expecting a higher number of visitors than we had in the Palais de Rumine, but we don't really know how much higher. In the Palais de Rumine we were one of four or five museums. We occupied one wing and one floor of a larger, broader museum complex. With all due respect, I would compare our former situation to that of a multiplex movie theater with multiple screens, none of which have a specific identity other than the movie being shown. In the Palais de Rumine we were never really able to affirm a specific identity vis-à-vis the public because we were just part of a larger whole. Near the railway station, we have a building that is exclusively for the Museum. It will be part of the wider Platform 10 complex; there will be two other museums opening later on, but that will certainly increase public interest in the Museum of Fine Arts. While new museums generally have a drop in their attendance after the first two years, the opening of the other institutions on the site should allow us to prolong the period of discovery that is translated in higher visitor numbers.

PJ: What advantages do you see in the new site as compared to your earlier location?

BF: I am convinced that the very fact of having our own building, and thus our own identity, will increase visitor numbers well beyond those that we had at the Palais de Rumine. Then too, we are located in a strategic part of the city, near the railway station, which certainly increases potential visitor numbers. In fact, the number of travelers passing through the station is slated to increase quite substantially in the next ten to fifteen years. The very large expansion plans of the station mean that there will be a work site near the Museum for several years, and if the entrance to Platform 10 is not clearly indicated, we may have to count that as a negative element in our visitor numbers. Clearly, it is difficult to predict visitor numbers with great accuracy over time, but all things considered we would obviously be disappointed if attendance did not increase substantially as compared with the recent Palais de Rumine period. We know that we had roughly one-third of our visitors who came from Lausanne and its region, one-third Swiss from other areas of the country, and one-third foreigners.

PJ: You publicly expressed your support for the earlier proposed museum location in Bellerive near the lake. How does that square with your position today?

BF: I was originally hired to be the first director of the Museum that was planned at Bellerive and I was favorable to that project. It became quickly apparent that so many negative things were written about the scheme that it would be difficult to build it. I still feel that it was a good design and that it would have made a viable museum. When a vote was held on the financing and the project lost, I was honestly very disappointed. I seriously considered leaving Lausanne. But the politicians involved reacted quickly. They had a public opinion poll taken to see if the population was really against a new museum, or primarily against the Bellerive project. A substantial majority expressed themselves in favor of a new building, but on another site, that was of course still to be chosen at that time. I was a member of the commission that was called on to examine potential locations, and I found that the railway station site was a good solution. Obviously, the other interesting solution was the Place de la Riponne, in front of the Palais de Rumine. There was, however, concern that such a visible and central site would again elicit broad opposition, whereas a railway yard site would be less sensitive from the point of view of public opinion. In any case, the Platform 10 site near the station offers a potential for much higher visitor numbers than Bellerive.

PJ: You were a member of the jury that selected Barozzi Veiga as the architects for the new Museum. Were you immediately convinced by their design?

BF: Although they were essentially unknown, I found that the scheme of Barozzi Veiga was an obvious choice. All of the functional elements of the project were in the right places. Very few changes were made between the competition entry and the final design. Barozzi Veiga worked with an excellent museum planner from Vienna called Dieter Bogner (bogner.knoll). I said to myself that the competition entry was a museum that could be built as it was designed and used directly in that form, which shows an unusual level of competence at that phase. In architectural terms, I was very favorable to the project because of its radicality.

PJ: It is said that the design of the new building is rather austere. Might that have to do with the very character of the Canton of Vaud and its people. Is there something Protestant about the design?

BF: The architects are from Catholic countries, Italy and Spain. I know that there have been references to the austerity of the architecture. In the company of visitors before the opening, as we walked along the north side with its brick fins and openings that only progressively become visible, the most frequent reaction was: “Wow, it’s impressive!” There is something archaic about the form of the building in my mind that recalls the feeling that one has seeing the pyramids in Egypt. The form is so simple, so basic, and yes, so beautiful that when I see this building, I have precisely that impression. If you just think of gray bricks, the first impression might be negative, but when you see the bricks up close and notice that they are all different, you perceive the work of the people who placed one brick after another. The joints are different from one fin to the next and that creates a kind of unity in the presence of diversity that is truly impressive. I would go so far as to say that there is sensuality in the way the materials of the building have been chosen and treated. I think many visitors are very sensitive to these aspects of the architecture. Once people are inside, they are taken in and awed by the entry hall and the main exhibition galleries. Certainly a first impression can be one of considerable austerity but looking closer, going inside, visitors appropriate the building to themselves.

PJ: The design of the entrance on the north side of the Museum is unexpected is it not?

BF: One can say that the entrance sequence with its rather monumental stairway is the *pièce de résistance* of the architects in terms of the overall Museum design. The reaction of visitors is conditioned by the 145-meter-long, 20-meter-high rectangular form of the structure. The entry is really the only powerful vertical element in the design. The entrance is placed where it is not only for its effect, but also because it intentionally separates the building in two with the permanent collections on one side and the temporary exhibitions on the other. The placement of the entry allows for relatively easy access to all parts of the Museum. In an unexpected and perhaps unplanned way, this sequence is reminiscent of the old Palais de Rumine, which is also divided in two by its monumental staircase and central entry point.

PJ: What is the work of art that you chose to place in the entry?

BF: We decided to place a single, monumental work of art in the entry. There were some practical considerations because the piece had to be fire resistant for security reasons, and because of its size. When Alice Pauli bought this 2011 work by Giuseppe Penone called *Luce e ombra* ("Light and Shadow"), she asked me if there was a place for it in the Museum, and it immediately seemed to me that there was only one logical place to put it. It has a limited footprint. Its form becomes more ample as it rises, symbolizing the arts and the contents of the Museum, with its play on light and shadow. *Luce* is symbolized by golden leaves that are amalgamated in a spherical form between four and five meters above the ground and *Ombra* is a granite sphere at the top of the work.

PJ: The main exhibition galleries are all designed to admit natural overhead light. Was that your wish?

BF: The competition program required that the upper-level galleries have natural overhead lighting. The largest exhibition gallery measures 700 square meters.

The overhead lighting can be entirely blocked if we wish, or we can admit full northern light, if the works allow, of course with no direct sunlight. The overhead lighting is also a form of comfort for visitors. In the presence of daylight, one is directly connected to the outside world. Closed into what I would call a catacomb, the visitor is ill at ease, this is a physiological fact. Recent museums like the extension of the Kunstmuseum in Basel by Christ & Gantenbein and the upcoming extension of the Kunsthaus in Zurich by David Chipperfield both have natural overhead lighting in the upper galleries. Renzo Piano's Beyeler Foundation building in Riehen (Basel) has magnificent natural overhead lighting.

PJ: Did the overhead lighting require a great deal of study and work beyond the phase of the competition entry?

BF: Absolutely. Achieving correct levels of natural light in museum galleries is very complex. There is an inherent paradox in the process. We feel as though we want as much natural light as possible to see the works, but the works themselves often need to be protected from excessive light. You have to find the correct point of balance and that is a difficult and highly technical task.

PJ: You have a single 700-square-meter gallery with a ceiling height of 5.5 meters. Is that likely to be a problem for the exhibition of small format works?

BF: In my opinion, there is no problem of scale. I have seen very small works of art exhibited to great effect in relatively vast spaces. What is an issue is the scenography for each exhibition. In Basel, for example, the new extension has relatively small spaces with real walls. This makes it difficult to create a specific exhibition design but means that shows can be changed rapidly. In our large gallery, we will have a down time of four weeks between exhibitions, which is the time required to demolish temporary walls and to create a new design. For certain projects, we will work with outside exhibition designers.

PJ: There are almost no views of the lake from the Museum, and yet the lake is magnificent. Is it not a little odd to cut the building off from its natural context?

BF: The building is, indeed, a kind of barrier between the train tracks and the north of the city. It is a kind of magnificent blank wall. The wall serves a protective function of course. The building in fact turns its back to the south where the lake is located, but from that direction, there could be no question of admitting direct sunlight. There were also security considerations on the south because of the possibility of hazardous cargoes being carried by freight trains. There never was any question, for example, of building a panoramic restaurant on the roof. That would have meant giving up part of the natural lighting scheme. Then too, the Elysée / mudac building will provide a view of the lake. Sure some people might regret that we don't have the best restaurant with a beautiful view of the lake but our goal was, above all, to build a twenty-first-century museum.

PJ: The Museum is located directly next to the railway tracks and some aspects of its design could be considered to be a reference to early twentieth-century industrial architecture for example. Does that reference seem correct?

BF: There is little or no industrial brick architecture in Lausanne or its region. I do see a relation to other museums such as the Gemeentemuseum in the Hague by H. P. Berlage (1931–35), built with yellow bricks, or Peter Zumthor's Kolumba Museum (Cologne, 2007), which uses gray brick as well.

PJ: You say that the design of the Museum is not necessarily related to the Protestant ethic, but, clearly, the jury sought a very restrained form of architectural expression?

BF: I would not say that we wanted a project that was restrained nor fundamentally austere. It is, on the contrary, generous. Even if it is not monumental in terms of the number of cubic meters, it creates an impression of monumentality from the exterior because of the length of the building. The perspective view on the northern side where the entrance and esplanade are located is impressive. The structure and material aspect of the façades are, indeed, restrained, but what can I say, it is a museum. There are various museum typologies, but take the example of the extension of the Mannheim Kunsthalle (von Gerkan Marg & Partners, 2018): it is a large, cubic composition that contains closed spaces that are linked together. This is the type of museum that is apparently very open both in the direction of the city and of the older building (1907). Among recent, "open" museums, one can also cite the Louvre Abu Dhabi (Jean Nouvel, 2017). And, conceived in a different way, there are inward-looking museums, such as the extension to the Basel Kunstmuseum (Christ & Gantenbein, 2016), or our own Museum. On the ground floor of our Museum there are frequent windows that serve to create a real link with the esplanade. As you go up in the building, the focus is naturally on the exhibition spaces and not on the view.

↓

Pierre Soulages
Peinture, 324 x 362 cm (Polyptyque J), 1987
Oil on canvas
324 x 362 cm (127.5 x 142.5 inches)

Works of Art in a Work of Architecture

Outrenoir. Beyond Black. Speaking of his entirely black paintings, the French artist Pierre Soulages said: "Outrenoir is another world where one can be transported by the reflection of light on a black surface, which is the greatest absence of light." More traditionally, a painting is like a window into another world, be it a mythological scene or an abstraction. A black painting by Pierre Soulages is not a window, but instead a kind of absorbing reflection. As dark and dense as they may be, his *outrenoir* paintings are an invitation to explore—art, but also perception, and ultimately oneself. Where opacity is the apparent quality of a surface, it may be that there are worlds to discover within, and beyond the first impression. This is a fundamental modern idea that is applicable to other forms of expression. The French philosopher Maurice Merleau-Ponty wrote: "With effort, I create an exploratory body dedicated to things and to the world, of such sensitivity that it becomes invested in me to the most profound recesses of myself and draws me immediately to the quality of space, from space to the object, and from the object to the horizon of all things, which is to say a world that is already there, that my relationship with being is formed."[2] These words, of broader philosophical import, can of course be applied to perception and thus to the understanding of art, and of architecture as well. It is only in modernity and abstraction that an entirely black painting can be understood for what it is today, a sign to look further, to see the light. Not an unfortunate imitation of the past, but, instead, an invitation to see.

[2] Maurice Merleau-Ponty, *Phénoménologie de la Perception*, Gallimard, Paris, 1976.

Like a black canvas, a blank wall might appear to invite no further thought nor any introspection. Seen more closely, its slightly irregular gray-brick surface is neither defensive nor designed to exclude. Rather it is the somewhat ambiguous sign of what lies within, "a world that is already there." This wall is devoid of decoration or even of windows; it is like a modern, monochromatic canvas. There is neither hubris nor fear in this wall; it is, instead, a contemporary gesture to architectural abstraction, a fundamentally simple and unpretentious presence—undeniable, and somehow ready to be approached and passed through, if not with the eyes and body, then with an open spirit. Architecture, like painting, has entered a time when modernity opens new possibilities, verging on abstraction, but also rooted in perception and thought, values that are timeless.

The new Museum of Fine Arts, Lausanne is unexpected. First, it is located almost directly next to railway tracks and the station. This is not the first museum to have been erected in such a place. The Art Institute of Chicago (Shepley, Rutan and Coolidge, 1893) was actually built over open-air railway tracks. More recently, the Museum Ludwig in Cologne (Peter Busmann, Godfrid Haberer, 1986) is close both to the station and to the Cathedral. The Hamburger Bahnhof in Berlin, originally built as a railway station in 1847, was repurposed by the architect Josef Paul Kleihues and became a contemporary art museum in 1997. Shigeru Ban's Centre Pompidou-Metz (2010) is also quite near the Metz station. And yet, in Lausanne, the Museum is so close to the tracks as to be a part of the train yard, or at least on the site of the former locomotive maintenance sheds. This location imposed a certain number of precautions against potential risks that might be posed by a derailed freight train for example. From the outset, it was clear the building would be solid and have few openings on its southern façade, facing the rails. Here none of the evanescent transparency seen in museums like the Louvre Lens (SANAA, Lens, 2012) would be possible.

Though somewhat larger than Lausanne, the Spanish city of Bilbao had confronted a similar situation when it decided to build a museum partially under a busy bridge at the river's edge. Frank O. Gehry's Guggenheim Bilbao, which opened in 1997, is frequently cited as an example of how a spectacular cultural building can almost literally transform a city, attracting tourism and worldwide attention.

Lausanne is not Bilbao however, and more than twenty years have gone by since the press and visitors first marveled at Gehry's exuberant titanium-clad forms. Emmanuel Ventura, the Cantonal architect of Vaud who has overseen the construction of the new Lausanne Museum, is well placed to explain the attitude of the region to this substantial cultural project. Without flinching, he calls the Swiss project, "the anti-Bilbao." The mentality of the Canton is such that there could be no question of investing 80 million francs (roughly equivalent to the same value in dollars) in a building that might seem extravagant. This attitude may well find its origin in the Protestant heritage of the region. Emmanuel Ventura explains: "Cities around the world launched architectural competitions for museums in the hope that they would suddenly find tourists streaming in. This trend was even called the 'Bilbao effect.' There was criticism in the architectural world of museums that were designed only for the sake of appearance. We were aware of this and we thought about it. I am reminded of a song by the Swiss author Jean Villard-Gilles called *Y en a point comme nous* ('Nobody Quite Like Us') that refers to the character and the modesty of the inhabitants of the Canton of Vaud. And he says those words with a strong local accent. In fact, I think we actively cultivate the idea that there is 'nobody quite like us.' In this instance, we looked at a place like Bilbao and said, well, they allowed themselves this gesture, but it is not for us to try to do the same, even if we are spending more than Bilbao did at the time. It is of course true that the jury was not made up entirely of people from the region, but when you pick jury members, you look also for people of like mind. To be quite direct, this is an anti-Bilbao. We did not want to do what others have done or tried to do. I am convinced that this sentiment is rooted in the Canton of Vaud and Protestant in its ethical view. One does see recent and austere museum buildings in Basel (Christ & Gantenbein, 2016) and in Chur where Barozzi Veiga also worked. It may be that this understatement or austerity is a Swiss phenomenon, as well as being strongly underscored in Lausanne by particular, local history and thought. Zaha Hadid won the competition for the Neues Stadt Casino in Basel (2003), but, in 2007, the citizens of Basel voted to halt the project."

In Lausanne, there was thus an almost conscious rejection of what was called the Bilbao effect. Here, there would be no sculptural excess. The result is a building that does indeed project an image of austerity, if only by its largely blank gray-brick walls. There is nonetheless a materiality in the building that its director calls sensual. The essentially rectangular structure is 145.5 meters long, 21.5 meters wide, and 22 meters high. Its eastern wall, facing the railway station, and the symmetrical counterpart to the west are uninterrupted 475-square-meter brick surfaces that can be considered austere, ambiguous, or perhaps mysterious in their monumental uniformity. The southern face of the building, clearly visible from trains entering from the direction of Paris or Geneva, has an extrusion corresponding to an element of the historic CFF locomotive sheds that were located on the site. The large, semicircular window seen here corresponds to the entrance lobby of the Museum, which is approached from the opposite, northern side. Only one other window, at the top of the second public stairway in the building, pierces the brick continuity of the railway track side of the Museum.

The northern façade of the Museum of Fine Arts, Lausanne is the most architecturally animated, forming one side of the new public esplanade that leads from the railway station toward the future Elysée / mudac museums for photography and design. This very straight 145.5-meter-long surface has a real rhythm, imposed by eighty-four pilasters separated by 151-centimeter gaps. The architect Alberto Veiga explains that these pilasters are an indirect reference to the neighboring railway tracks and their rigorously spaced ties. Veiga also makes a convincing case for the transition from the totally blank eastern façade to this northern sequence, which contains not only the public entrance, framed in a strict concrete box, but also a succession of ground-floor windows. The windows reveal bits of the activity inside, a book and gift shop, a cafeteria, an auditorium, and an informal art project space. Nine other irregularly placed rectangular windows pierce the façade on the two upper levels, allowing light into galleries or public spaces. These windows are all divided by the brick-covered pilasters. Glowing from within in the darker hours, the Museum cedes some of its mystery to passersby, and contributes to what the architects imagine as a cultural street in the midst of Platform 10, but also a kind of wall, protecting the esplanade from the railway lines. Opposite the northern façade of the Museum, existing stone arcades have been converted into usable spaces for workshops and a café. Concern over the risks to the building, the works of art, and visitors were thus obviated by the very nature of the design, which intentionally forms a barrier between the railway tracks and the public square to the north.

The pervasive grayness of the new Museum is undoubtedly more than an aesthetic whim of the architects. They feel, certainly with reason, that their choice is rooted in this place. And also because of the length and breadth of the surfaces, finding a brick that could give form to their perception of Lausanne was not simple. In a short 1981 movie about Lausanne called *Lettre à Freddy Buache*, the Franco-Swiss filmmaker Jean-Luc Godard referred to filming meaning the forest above, the lake below, and the gray city in between. Freddy Buache, the founder of the Swiss Film Archive (Cinémathèque), was, coincidentally, one of the leaders of the group opposed to the Bellerive site for the new museum.

Like Barozzi Veiga almost forty years later, Godard seized on an essence, an identity that is visual but perhaps, more deeply, contextual. Translating this perception of the city into built form was not as easy as it might seem. The choice of the bricks used in the building was the object of intensive study and debate. The architects were very much in favor of bricks that would have some irregularity, that would resemble the work of artisans, to give life to the façades. The bricks chosen were made with a process that was practically invented for this building. "We are very pleased with the way these bricks appear under local lighting conditions and on such large surfaces. What seems like a very simple part of the process was in fact the result of a huge amount of work," explains Emmanuel Ventura.

Visitors enter the Museum through glass and stainless-steel doors that are relatively modest as compared to the vast length of the building. Inside, the most spectacular architectural element of the edifice is immediately visible. The high concrete space of the lobby, with skylights above and the semicircular window of the old locomotive sheds directly opposite the entrance doors, is bright but constrained in its width. The full southern side of the lobby is marked by stairs that rise up to the window that allows a direct view onto the neighboring railway tracks. This gesture situates the Museum in time and space, underlining what Alberto Veiga calls the soul of the city. The steps were conceived to serve as seating, especially in case of any event organized in the lobby. The interest and strength of the work of the architects is confirmed by this space, which is functional—leading right and left into public spaces, and above into the galleries—but also unexpectedly monumental. Like the building itself which is not truly massive, but nonetheless projects a kind of undeniable monumentality, this lobby sequence is not grand in the exuberant sense, but, instead, conducive to a contemplative mood. This is not a temple space but, with the stairs leading to the light (and, more practically, to the galleries), it is a place to enter with respect. The entire building—the façades and this lobby in particular—is solid, stony, hard. The lobby is the modest door that leads to discovery. It is the only way for visitors to pass into the wall-like building, but once through the doors, visitors can look to the sky and be bathed in light. This could well be seen as a kind of symbolic epiphany were it not that, here, the galleries remain to be discovered by entering visitors. And it is precisely not an epiphany because the architects have resolved that their work is not in itself the art; their task is, instead, to make the art visible, and to show it in the best possible conditions. Continuous terrazzo floors and steps inside the lobby give a strong feeling of continuity to the space, as do the high walls finished in lime plaster. This is where Ventura's idea of the "anti-Bilbao" takes on its meaning. Barozzi Veiga did not take it upon themselves to create a sculptural art form; instead they adapted strict, stony lines of rigorous forms, from the façades to the lobby.

The *raison d'être* of the building, at least inside, is indeed to show works of art, in any way that the curators, present and future, will wish to do so. The galleries are arrayed on the two upper floors of the building, with some lateral northern windows that can be covered with curtains on the first floor, and above, a glorious array of overhead natural lighting, complemented as required by artificial light sources. Floors are in terrazzo on the ground and first levels and in oak on the top level. Walls are white and ceilings high, reaching up 5.5 meters, giving an impression of freedom and space. All the galleries can be divided at least in two with temporary walls designed for the purpose. The *pièce de résistance* of the gallery sequence is the main space on the eastern, second story of the building. Here the 700-square-meter volume can be divided in four for temporary exhibitions, but is also available as a single, sweeping gesture that few other contemporary museums can offer. This gallery offers no windows but does have ample natural light.

The point is clearly not to glorify the building itself, or even its architects, nor even the possible views. As Bernard Fibicher, the director, says, *this is a museum.* This affirmation might seem quite obvious, but in the face of so many institutions that have privileged architectural gestures over their own collections, Fibicher's words ring like a simple affirmation of an underlying fact. This is a museum. Ground-floor facilities of course provide an ample shop, an event space for art, auditorium and café, but there is neither a luxurious restaurant, nor even permanent seating in the auditorium. These public areas, like the galleries themselves, can be adapted and changed in the future; they are rectangular boxes with windows that look out to the north toward the public square. They are meant to be animated and filled with life. The nature of that animation has not been dictated by architectural whims nor by extravagant forms—the public spaces, like the galleries themselves, are high and generous, made for the comfort of visitors and users. Confirming what seems obvious inside the building, Emmanuel Ventura states: "I think that visitors will understand that in Lausanne this building serves a clear purpose. Inside, the galleries are carefully and thoughtfully designed to receive works of art with respect. There is natural overhead lighting, 5.5-meter-high ceilings, ideal conditions for viewing wonderful works. What might be called architectural gesticulation would not be respectful of the art."

Alberto Veiga calls the railway tracks at this precise place "the soul of the city." This affirmation also speaks to the very reason that the Museum is located where it is. A clear reason for the political decision taken to place the new Platform 10 complex near the railway station was the upcoming expansion of the station itself and its environment. Current passenger flows of 140,000 persons per day are due to increase in the coming years to 200,000 persons per day, creating a ready pool of potential visitors. Aside from the Platform 10 architectural competitions, there was one for the renovation and expansion of the station, and another for the development area to the east, which is called La Rasude. Presently occupied by the railway company and the Post Office, this large tract of land on the opposite side of the railway station from Platform 10 has now been slated for a large residential, retail, and hotel area. This project is due for 2025 completion, as should be the case for the station expansion. The French architects TVK, who had previously transformed the Place de la République in Paris, won the competition for the upgrading of the square in front of the station. These developments place the new Museum of Fine Arts, but also the whole of Platform 10, in the perspective of a very substantial development of Lausanne. From its location in a neo-Renaissance palace, the Museum of Fine Arts has taken on a new place in the heart of the active city that Lausanne is becoming.

The brick façade of the Museum of Fine Arts, Lausanne that faces the railway station is, in fact, an architectural gesture. The lack of ornament or fenestration immediately makes this façade enigmatic. Its scale is not apparent from a distance—the matter of size is resolved only when the visitor approaches, a first step to passing through the wall in a metaphorical, if not literal, sense. And so yes, even up close, a 22-meter-high brick wall looks big, and is imbued with a sense of monumentality even if the building that it forms in space is not out of scale. There is a monumentality expressed here that is actually in perfect proportion with the city, with the site, and with the function. One might call it a monumental simplicity. Austerity is a word that can be applied to this architecture, but surely more appropriate is the term simplicity. The barrier that the Museum forms between the tracks and the new public square of Platform 10 defines and protects the space. And in the middle of this long wall, the modest but well-proportioned entrance actively continues the image of modesty that imbues the whole of this architectural object. And yes, the function of the building is quite literally what inhabits this "wall," this closed but progressively more and more open object. Inside, a lobby that invites pause and reflection, but more, galleries that are free of gesticulation and complexity. Simplicity is the rule.

In his well-known treatise on Japanese traditional architecture, *In Praise of Shadows* (1933), Junichiro Tanazaki writes: "In the mansion called literature I would have the eaves deep and the walls dark, I would push back into the shadows the things that come forward too clearly, I would strip away the useless decoration. I do not ask that this be done everywhere, but perhaps we may be allowed at least one mansion where we can turn off the electric lights and see what it is like without them." The Museum of Fine Arts, Lausanne is not a place of overhanging eaves or dark walls. It is a place where the light is within, where one can "turn off the electric lights and see what it is like without them." There are other museums that rely on simplicity of course, but in this instance, there is a conjugation of modesty, appropriate monumentality, and above all a deep-seated understanding of what modernity means today. Not all visitors will be able or willing to penetrate what presents itself as a completely black canvas or a blank wall, but there is a place for those persons too in this Museum. One can look at a work, or even just at the railway tracks and leave; one can have a coffee in the square and then move on. Or one can pass through the stone walls in a metaphorical and intellectual sense to discover "visions of the past and visions of the future." Merleau-Ponty further wrote:

What is indefinable in the *quale*[3], in color, is nothing other than a rapid and peremptory way to give a single something, a shade of the being, whole clusters of visions of the past and visions of the future. I, who see, have my depth as well, I am linked to the same visible existence that I see, and that closes up behind me even as I pass, I know very well. The density of the body is not in rivalry with that of the world, on the contrary, it is the only way to go to the heart of things, in making myself the world and making things flesh.

[3] A *quale* can be defined in very summary terms as "intrinsic non-representational" property. See http://plato.stanford.edu/entries/qualia/ accessed on February 15, 2019.

Maurice Merleau-Ponty,
Le visible et l'invisible (The Visible and the Invisible), 1964

→
The blank eastern façade of the Museum is an unexpected invitation to discover what lies within

Events and Performances

The director of the Museum, Bernard Fibicher, has wanted to have artists associated with every phase of the new Museum's creation. He reached out to artists with whom the Museum has had strong connections, such as Ai Wei Wei and Markus Raetz, asking them to give very small objects (less than 5 cubic cm) that were to be placed in a box laid in the ground with the cornerstone of the building on October 6, 2016. Also included in the box, works by artists who had passed away, symbolizing the links between the Museum of the future and its own past—a brush that belonged to Balthus and a painting knife of Zao Wu Ki donated by their widows, as well as the charred plaque of Gleyre's *Execution of Major Davel*, the work destroyed by an arsonist in 1980.

In the spirit of this close relationship between the building and its artists, and underlining an openness to the contemporary creative world, Bernard Fibicher also organized a brief exhibition in the work site of the new Museum between August 31 and September 9, 2018. *Robert Wilson Balthus Unfinished* was a show devoted to unfinished works by Balthus (Balthazar Klossowski de Rola, 1908–2001). In low light, visitors were allowed to come into the Museum through the service entrance, and from there to take the freight elevator, not up into the galleries, but down into the future reserves. Eighteen unfinished paintings and drawings of Balthus were exhibited in a carefully lit, musically animated, theatrical space, "on display in a building that is unfinished—under construction—itself." Born in 1941, Robert Wilson is an American playwright and stage director who has often worked on exhibitions of art. In 1992, *The New York Times* described him as "America's, or even the world's, foremost vanguard theater artist." Unexpected, even disturbing for some, *Robert Wilson Balthus Unfinished* was an invitation to see art anew, to look at works that are not what they seem again, and also to open the spirit of visitors to installations that cross over the normal frontiers between painting and theater. The preface of this book is an original work (and text) by Robert Wilson.

On April 6 and 7, 2019, when construction had finished, the Museum opened its doors. Organized before works from the collection had been hung in the galleries, this was an occasion for the public to discover the spaces, but also to enjoy performances by such varied groups as the Swiss association of young authors, the Collectif Ajar, the musicians of the Ensemble Batida, the noted French artist Pierre Huyghe, or the theater artist Christophe Jacquet. Again, as in the installation by Robert Wilson, a clear message was given: the Museum of Fine Arts, Lausanne would not be a staid place for painting and sculpture but, instead, a living institution open to its environment and to changing views about art.

↑
The exhibition *Robert Wilson Balthus Unfinished* was held in the basement of the work site of the Museum between August 31 and September 9, 2018

→

The entire Museum opened to the public without any works of art in place on April 6 and 7, 2019

A Crocodile Arrives

As was the case for the architecture of the two museums on the Platform 10 site, an international competition was organized for a commissioned work of art to be placed on the esplanade between the two buildings. Since 1979 the Canton of Vaud has systematically organized competitions for public buildings to select works of art that give a "character to a building or enhance its architecture." This so-called "art and architecture" initiative was made official in an April 1, 2015, regulation (Règlement concernant l'intervention artistique sur les batiments de l'Etat RIABE) that stipulates that the sums allotted are in proportion to construction costs for the building concerned. It is further directed that where possible a collaboration between the artists and the architects involved should be established. The goal here was to select "a work of art that engages the urban and museum context in a coherent way, taking into account their public nature."

The competition was announced on September 9, 2016. Seventy-three proposals were received, of which twenty-one were retained for the second phase of the work related to the Museum of Fine Arts. The jury president was Emmanuel Ventura, the Cantonal architect. Members of the jury included the directors of the three museums that are to be located on the site, as well as the architects Fabrizio Barozzi and Manuel Aires Mateus. The winning proposal was the work *Crocodile*, conceived by the artists Olivier Mosset and Xavier Veilhan, who came together specifically for this competition. Olivier Mosset, born in 1944 in Bern, is a painter and sculptor who lives in Tucson, Arizona. Xavier Veilhan, born in 1963, is a French painter, sculptor, and installation artist. Their monumental 18-meter-long work in painted metal was inspired by the well-known Swiss 6/8II locomotive, produced beginning in 1919 and known as the Crocodile because of its unusual form. As they explain, the artists were intrigued by the juxtaposition of a machine produced at the beginning of the era of electric locomotives with the name of an aggressive aquatic reptile. The stylized lines of their work immediately bring to mind the railyard context of Platform 10. According to the official report on the competition: "The jury was nearly unanimous in recognizing the iconic aspect of the proposal and its strong link to the history of the site and the scale of the buildings. The quality of the collaboration between the artists was also noted—they were able to put aside the normally solitary nature of their artistic engagement in order to produce a shared work on a large scale."

Urban Furniture—Mobile and Anchored

The overall site of Platform 10 has a good deal of open space, where the *Crocodile* designed by Olivier Mosset and Xavier Veilhan will be placed. A competition for the design of this space and the requisite urban furniture was organized in 2018. Seven groups were invited to participate: Big-Game (Lausanne); Jörg Boner (Zurich); ECAL (Renens); Adrien Gardère (Paris); INCH Furniture (Basel); Adrien Rovero (Lausanne); and Marco Sousa Santos (Lisbon). The jury deliberated in October and November 2018, and was presided by Emmanuel Ventura, the Cantonal architect, and Chantal Prod'Hom, the director of the mudac. It also included the directors of the other two museums on the site, and the architects Fabrizio Barozzi and Manuel Aires Mateus. For the urban furniture, INCH was selected. INCH has worked on such projects as the "City Lounge" furniture for Art Basel (2016–18), and furnishings for the extension of the Swiss National Museum by Christ & Gantenbein (Zurich, 2016). Their proposal consisted in a number of elements to be disposed in peripheral locations near the open spaces. Described by the jury as an "anti-thesis of urban furniture," many of the objects have a rounded or lens-like form 2.5 by 5.5 meters in diameter. These groups of concrete and wood benches or rather podiums can be used for many different purposes and are complemented by gray light poles, trash cans, and bicycle racks.

A New Public Square for Lausanne

The masterplan for the entire square in front of the new Museum of Fine Arts and extending close to the future Elysée / mudac building by Aires Mateus was prepared by Barozzi Veiga. For the space directly adjoining the Museum, there is a line of gravel, and then there is a 25-centimeter concrete division. Beyond these bands the architects have employed a surface material made by shot blasting bituminous concrete with small pebbles (*enrobé grenaillé*), a kind of asphalt with stones in it which is stable and resistant even with heavy use. The former railway tracks leading into the site have been preserved, as has the preexisting concrete between the tracks. In front of the arcades there is again gravel in a honeycomb metal structure. The stone arcades have their original form and Barozzi Veiga added glass and stainless-steel façades. Trees planted along the arcades between the entrance and a stairway leading up to the Rue Ruchonnet, the only vegetation in the square, were selected in collaboration with the city. They are European hop-hornbeam trees (*Ostrya carpinifolia*), a native broadleaf deciduous tree that can reach up to 14 meters in height. When Aires Mateus was selected for the photography and design museum, the architects worked together to make slight changes in the surfaces near the second building, taking into account the fact that it is in concrete. The Rue Ruchonnet stairs on the northern side of the site were designed by Barozzi Veiga but built under the supervision of Aires Mateus. Barozzi Veiga also designed the mandatory 1.5-meter-high barrier separating the esplanade of the two museums from the railway track.

Photography and Design— Elysée/mudac

Another Architectural Competition

The second phase of the Platform 10 project concerned the new building dedicated to the Elysée (photography) and mudac (design) museums.

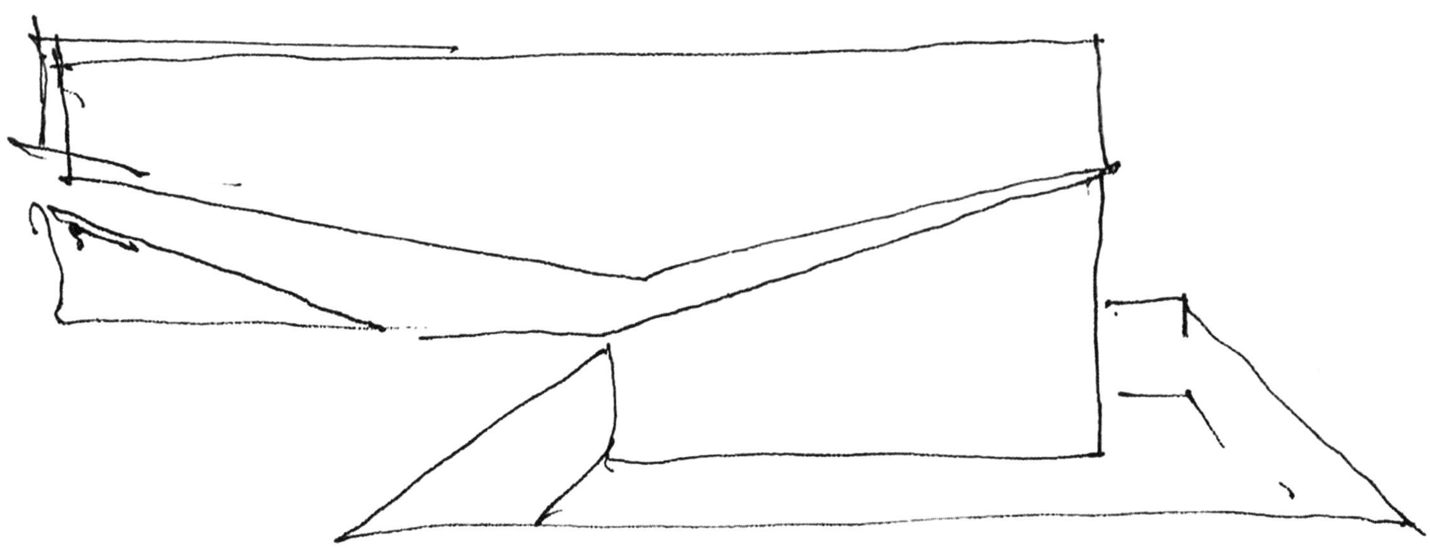

The competition for the architecture of the new building formally started on January 9, 2015, and 149 architectural offices expressed interest in participating. Like the jury for the Museum of Fine Arts, the group involved was presided over by Oliver Steimer, and included both David Chipperfield and Kengo Kuma as vice presidents. The respective museum directors Tatyana Franck (Elysée) and Chantal Prod'Hom (mudac) were also jury members, along with Fabrizio Barozzi and the Canton's architect Emmanuel Ventura. The jury selected twenty-one candidates from nine different countries. Among these were Jean Nouvel, Dominique Perrault, SANAA, Shigeru Ban, and Steven Holl. The Swiss teams Gigon/Guyer, Christ & Gantenbein, Peter Märkli, and Valerio Olgiati were also in the group picked for the second phase. On October 5, 2015, the jury announced the selection of the "One Museum, Two Museums" project by the talented team Aires Mateus from Lisbon. Whereas the original masterplan for the site imagined three buildings, the Portuguese architects made a convincing proposal to unite the two institutions in the same structure. On February 8, 2017, the Conseil d'Etat (Vaud) voted a CHF 51.8-million budget for the construction, and further funds for access roads and other expenses. The city of Lausanne transmitted the site to the Canton on August 30, 2017, and also voted a CHF 20-million credit for a part of the overall construction budget. The construction of the new building began on June 1, 2018. In terms of overall organization, a logical step for this substantial series of projects was taken when it was announced in February 2019 that the three museums would be grouped in a single entity, called the Platform 10 Foundation.

The visual identity of "Plateforme 10" (Platform 10), unveiled in 2016, was created by the art director Régis Tosetti, a graduate of Lausanne's ECAL, and Simon Palmieri, who was trained in Basel (Hochschule für Gestaltung und Kunst). The visual identity scheme evokes the ongoing links between the institutions on the site as well as the locomotive turntable which has been conserved at the entrance to the site. The Lausanne railway station has nine tracks, whence the reference to continuity in the form of a tenth (cultural) platform.

←
Sketch by Manuel Aires Mateus for the Elysée/mudac building

A Concrete Vision: Aires Mateus

The design of Manuel and Francisco Aires Mateus forms a single volume that nonetheless denotes the duality of the enterprise, with spaces devoted to the mudac design museum in the upper level and to the Elysée photography museum below.

A glazed horizontal "fissure" divides the institutions, bringing light to the interiors during the day and standing out in the evening. The architects describe it as an empty space that widens and contracts, serving as an entrance and a space of passage that is always in contact with the exterior, forming a covered plaza that gives access to both museums. The new building provides an exhibition space of 1,529 square meters for the mudac and 1,398 square meters for the Elysée museums with a shared entrance on the esplanade opposite the Museum of Fine Arts.

Manuel Rocha de Aires Mateus was born in Lisbon, Portugal, in 1963. He graduated as an architect from the Faculty of Architecture at the Technical University of Lisbon (FA-UTL; 1986). He worked with Gonçalo Byrne beginning in 1983 and with his brother Francisco Xavier Rocha de Aires Mateus beginning in 1988. Francisco Xavier de Aires Mateus was born in Lisbon in 1964. He also graduated from the FA-UTL (1987) and began working with Gonçalo Byrne in 1983, before his collaboration with his brother. Their work includes the Santa Marta Light House Museum (Cascais, 2003–07), a school complex (Vila Nova da Barquinha, 2006–08), EDP Headquarters, Portuguese Electric Company (Lisbon, 2008–09), Portugal Telecom Call Center (Santo Tirso, 2008–09), and numerous private houses including the House in Melides II (Melides, 2014–15). They won a competition to design a new addition and entrance to the Musée des Augustins in Toulouse (France, 2017). Another of their recent projects, the Muslim Center in Bordeaux (France, 2016–18) bears some intellectual comparison to the project for Lausanne. According to the architects, this building was "designed with a principle consisting in a compression between the pavement and the roof, between the 'sky' and the 'earth.' This principle defines the most symbolic space of both projects (Lausanne and Bordeaux). In the case of the Muslim Center, it had to do with designing the religious spaces in between the welcoming area and the teaching zone, using the limit of the three levels to create a form that strives to find a parallel between the horizontal—the relationship with men—and the vertical—the relationship with God."

Although their work sometimes appears to be simple, the Aires Mateus brothers bring a surprising depth and complexity to the forms and light that they use to create spaces that are modern and subtle. It may be that they prefer a lighter, whiter version of modernity than Barozzi Veiga, but the two teams actually share a profound interest in developing contemporary architecture that does not allow itself to become excessively expressive, while still mastering spatial surprise and fully usable volumes.

←

A rendering of the future Elysée/mudac building by Aires Mateus

Two Museums in One Building

The mudac was located in the seventeenth-century Gaudard House near the Cathedral. This residence was actually formed from several existing buildings.

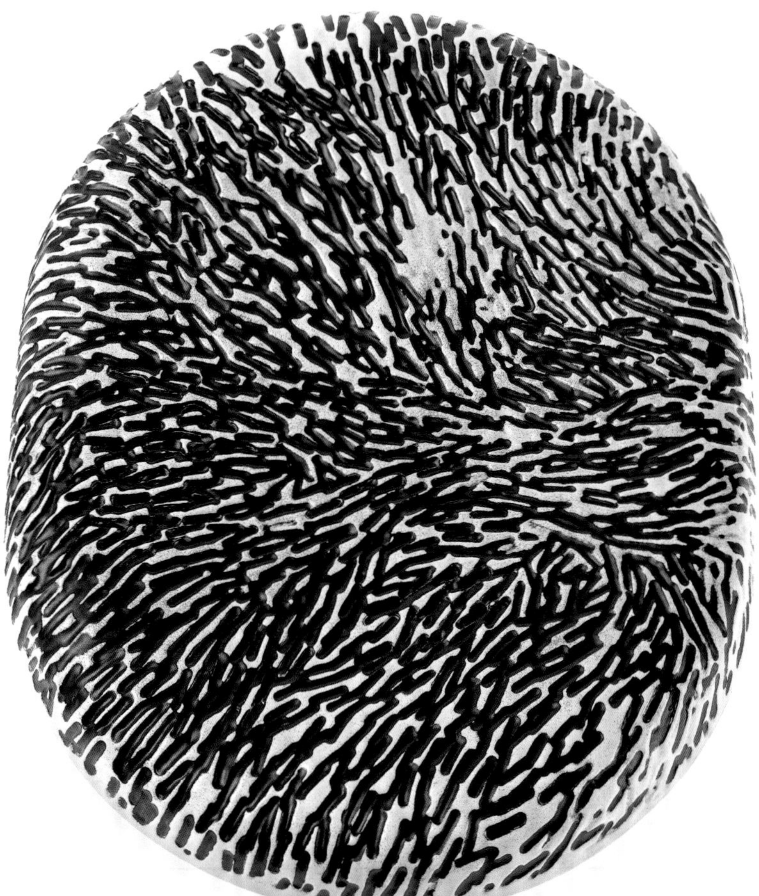

←

Dimitri Bähler
Small Oblong Plate
(Fur Patterns/Black on White Satin), 2013
Ceramic
26 x 20 x 2.5 cm (10.2 x 7.9 x 1 inches)

The northern portion of the current mudac edifice was built in the thirteenth century and was inhabited until 1340 by the goldsmith Perrot Dorer. Renovated by the architects Monod + Monod beginning in 1995, the mudac opened to the public in June 2000. The mudac collections include approximately 3,000 objects and is the only museum in French-speaking Switzerland exclusively dedicated to design and contemporary applied arts. More than 100 exhibitions were organized in the Gaudard House between 2000 and 2016. The limited floor space and complex configuration of an old house did not permit the mudac to show its collections in an appropriate manner. In the new building, a selection from the prestigious contemporary glass art collection, one of the most famous in the world, will be almost permanently on exhibition. The contemporary jewelry, ceramic, design, and print collections will be shown to the public on a rotating basis.

Founded in 1985 as a photography museum by the journalist and photographer Charles-Henri Favrod (1927–2017), the Musée de l'Elysée has been directed by Tatyana Franck since 2015. Internationally recognized, the Elysée Museum is one of the leading institutions of its type. Since its creation, the museum has presented innovative exhibitions accompanied by authoritative publications, and also organized events open to the general public. The collections of the museum include nearly a million photographic documents (prints, negatives, and contact sheets and slides) as well as 20,000 books. Groups of works by Ella Maillart, Marcel Imsand, Réné Burri, and Sabine Weiss are among the highlights of the collection. The museum has been housed in the elegant house built between 1780 and 1783 for the military officer Henri de Mollins (1729–1811) by the architect Abraham Fraisse. Purchased by the Canton in 1971 and renovated at that time, the building housed the print collections of the Canton, since then moved to Vevey. In its earlier years, the Elysée Museum focused on classical and historical images, but has since placed greater emphasis on contemporary creativity.

↓

<u>*Pieke Bergmans*</u>
Light Bulb (chair), 2015
Glass, metal, and LED
83 x 42 x 40 cm (32.7 x 16.5 x 15.7 inches)

↓

Hans Steiner
Piscine KaWeDe, Berne
(KaWeDe Swimming Pool, Bern), 1935–40
Gelatin silver bromide print
19.5 x 17.5 cm (7.6 x 6.8 inches)

The Future of the Site— Lausanne as a Cultural Destination

50
LAUSANNE
CH-SBB

Pascal Broulis

Head of the Department of Finance and Exterior Relations,
Etat de Vaud

Philip Jodidio: When was it decided that it was necessary to build a new Museum of Fine Arts in Lausanne?

Pascal Broulis: As early as 1924, the director of the Museum requested more space for exhibitions and the storage of works. In 1936, the Museum received the very substantial Widmer donation, began to open itself up more to international art, and at the same time started to organize temporary exhibitions. All of these factors made the lack of space even more obvious. Finally, in 1992, the State Council of Vaud made the decision to move the Museum of Fine Arts out of the Palais de Rumine. The first plan for a new museum involved the Bellerive area at Ouchy next to the lake, but, after funding for that location was rejected by referendum, the present site near the railway station was selected instead. At last outside of the Palais de Rumine, and in its own building, the Museum will be able to create an independent identity, something that has been lacking for more than a century.

PJ: Why was the site near the station selected?

PB: An analysis of the failure of the Bellerive project revealed that the public rejection was in good part related to the specific location concerned and the desire of voters to protect the shores of the lake. The will to build a new museum still existed. The State Council created a study group to evaluate other sites in the Canton. Eleven options were studied in detail, and the Council pronounced itself in favor of the large plot next to the Lausanne railway station. This choice was motivated by the proximity of a particularly dense public transport system. Within a few years, approximately 200,000 travelers will go through the station, which is equidistant from Milan and Paris, every day. The station also offers easy connections to the major cities of Switzerland—Geneva, Lucerne, Zurich, Basel or Bern—and is just forty minutes from the international airport in Geneva.

PJ: How would you describe the ambitions of the Platform 10 complex in the longer term, for example after 2025? Do you believe that tourism will substantially increase thanks to the new cultural facilities?

PB: Lausanne already has a considerable international reputation, which is rare for a city of its size. It is the headquarters city of the International Olympic Committee, and fifty other international sports federations are located in the Canton. The creation of Platform 10 is obviously an occasion to further increase the attractiveness of Lausanne and thus to develop tourism. Lausanne has more highly rated hotels and restaurants than just about any comparable European city and it offers an exceptional panoramic view of the lake and the Alps. It is a perfect destination for a magical weekend.

Cesla Amarelle

Head of the Department of Education, Youth and Culture,
Etat de Vaud

Philip Jodidio: Subsequent to the rejection of the Bellerive location, why did the Council of State choose the site of the former locomotive sheds at the railway station for the new museum?

Cesla Amarelle: A committee was tasked with evaluating the best possible sites in the Canton. Proximity to the railway station offers the clear advantage of easy access to the passenger flows going to and from the rest of the region, the country, and a number of European capitals. I am convinced that culture must be accessible to all, so I am fully in agreement with the choice of this site.

PJ: How was it decided to put not one but three museums on this site?

CA: The size of the site selected permitted a more ambitious approach. Another local institution with an international reputation, the Elysée Museum, was also housed in an old building with insufficient space. Partnership between the city of Lausanne and the Canton also allowed us to extend the new project to include the mudac design museum. The mudac is closely associated with ECAL, the school of art and design. The decision to have three museums on the site rapidly became evident.

PJ: What are the ambitions of the Platform 10 complex in the medium and longer terms? What balance do you see between the expenses engaged and the potential benefits of the overall project?

CA: This new cultural neighborhood brings three museums to one site, a situation that is unique in Switzerland. Events planned for the complex will encourage the convergence of other cultural areas as well. Platform 10 is in keeping with the ambitious goals of the cultural policy of the Canton. A new public square dedicated to the arts and to culture in the capital city of Vaud is nothing short of an urban revolution. The encouragement given to the arts is a significant element of local societal cohesion. Although it is clear that indirect benefits will accrue to the vicinity of the complex and the city, this is not only about financial benefits. The position of Lausanne as a city of culture will be substantially reinforced and the public will have easier access to the arts.

PJ: How will Platform 10 influence the younger population that your department favors? How can museums compete with the increasingly dominant attraction of Internet?

CA: Young people, just like the rest of the population, need a place for social interaction. Today's museums are no longer as discrete and calm as they used to be, they are lively places. The efforts that are already being made in the area of cultural mediation will be increased in partnership with schools. New pedagogical resources will be offered to teachers, and there will be services in the museums to receive school groups in the best conditions possible, including free entry. This will permit the museum to play its real role in society—to become a convivial place of exchange, sociability, and discussion. A museum must play a role in encouraging the cohesion of the overall population. Finally, I would say that seeing original works of art remains very important even in the era of Internet. This is a fundamental need that no virtual environment can replace.

↓ →
The underground spaces of the Museum include a state-of-the-art technical area (right) and the Museum reserves (below)

Olivier Steimer

President of the Council of the Foundation of the Museum of Fine Arts, Lausanne

Philip Jodidio: You were the president of the architectural juries for the Museum of Fine Arts and for the Elysée/mudac building. How did you come into these responsibilities?

Olivier Steimer: As president of the Cantonal Bank of Vaud (Banque Cantonal Vaudoise), I was called on to participate in the BUD Committee which had responsibilities for the construction of the University of Lausanne at Dorigny. It was in this context that I was first called on to preside over an architectural jury, for the Géopolis building in Dorigny in 2008. After the failure of the Bellerive site for the Museum, I participated from 2009 to 2010 in the Canton's evaluation group for the numerous proposed sites. Once the location at the railway station was chosen, I was asked to be the president of the jury for the new building.

PJ: What were your priorities as president of the jury?

OS: To organize and conduct the discussion in a manner that would include all the useful opinions but would also guarantee an efficient decision that would respect the objectives of the client. The issue was to choose an original and aesthetic architectural solution, with an optimal use of space in keeping with the functions of a museum, and to stay within the budget fixed by the State Council. Fortunately the jury, and in particular its vice president David Chipperfield, had perfectly understood the situation.

PJ: Is that the reasoning that led to the choice of Barozzi Veiga, an architectural team that was not very well known at the time?

OS: Absolutely. The eighteen projects and candidates selected for the second round were subsequently evaluated by the jury in a completely anonymous process that obliged all concerned to concentrate on the quality of the projects rather than on the reputation of the architects. We were all surprised when the name of Barozzi Veiga was revealed. The architects selected had made an audacious choice, that of demolishing the existing railway structure in order to create a new public space. Their scheme also left a place for the future Elysée and mudac museums. They found a way to create a highly functional museum without putting themselves forward. Not everyone can build a museum like the Guggenheim Bilbao, but would it even have been possible on this site?

PJ: What did you retain from the second competition for the Elysée/mudac building?

OS: The work of the jury went forward in much the same way as for the first building. With the assistance of the full jury and of Kengo Kuma, the vice president, we managed to select a project that satisfied the differing requirements of the two institutions, which are thus grouped together. Aires Mateus designed a very aesthetic building in complete harmony with its neighbor and also in keeping with the philosophy of this new cultural neighborhood. One of the winners, Francisco Aires Mateus, had been a member of the first jury and I believe that that permitted him to have a good understanding of the site and of the philosophy behind the project.

PJ: You are currently the president of the Council of the Foundation of the Museum of Fine Arts, Lausanne. On January 1, 2018, the Museum became a foundation under public law.

OS: The mission of the Foundation is to carry out the strategic cultural objectives of the Museum and to ensure that it is well managed. I was asked to continue my activity during this transition phase because I have a good deal of management experience in the private sector and because I know these projects quite well. The entire legal and administrative structure of the Museum has been changed, and new factors, such as a greatly increased schedule of temporary exhibitions and an increase in staff numbers, have emerged.

WOLFF
44
50

La Mobilière

Plans of the Museum

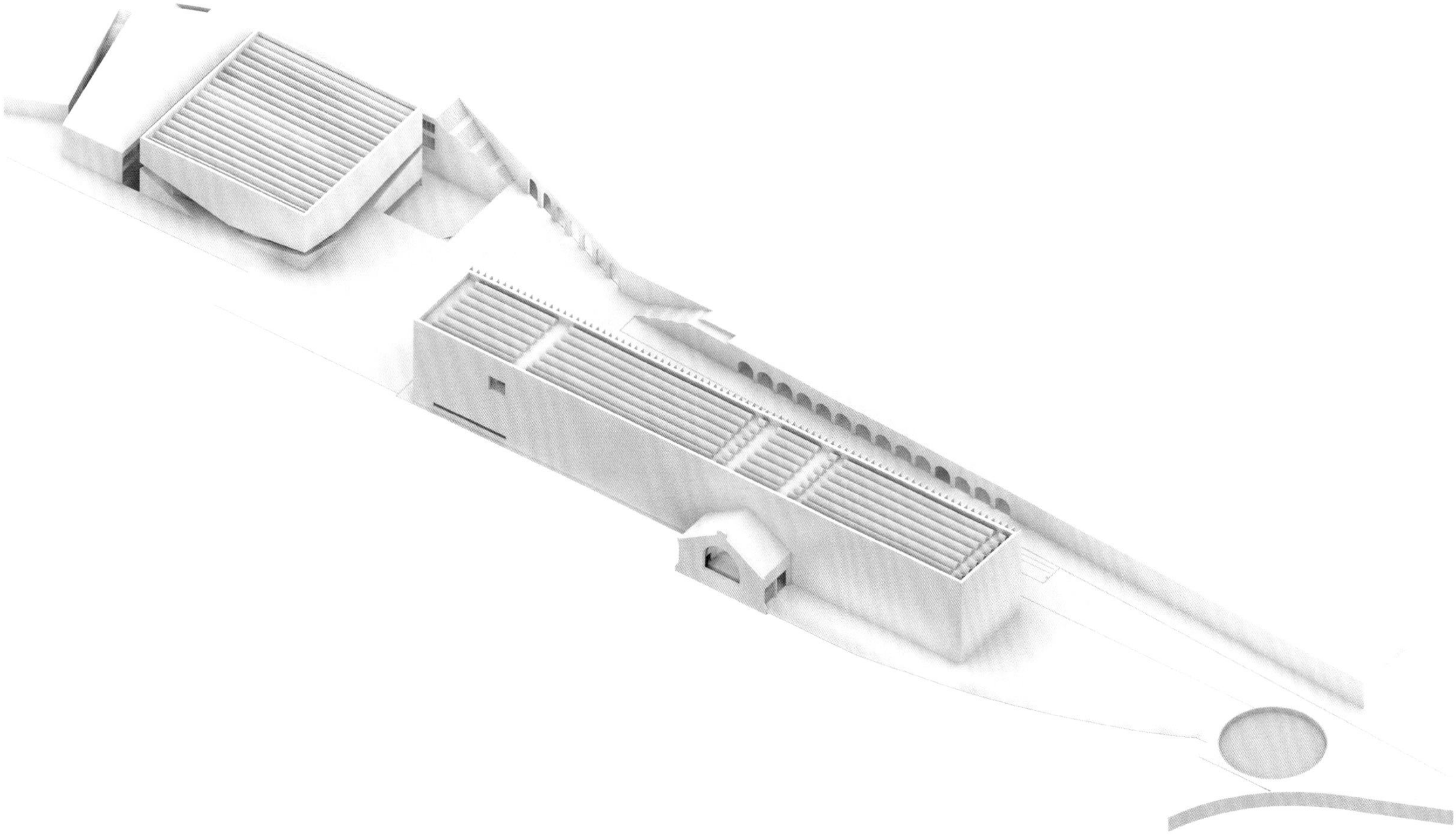

↑
Above, an axonometric view of the entire Platform 10 site including the Museum of Fine Arts and the future Elysée/mudac building

→
Second floor

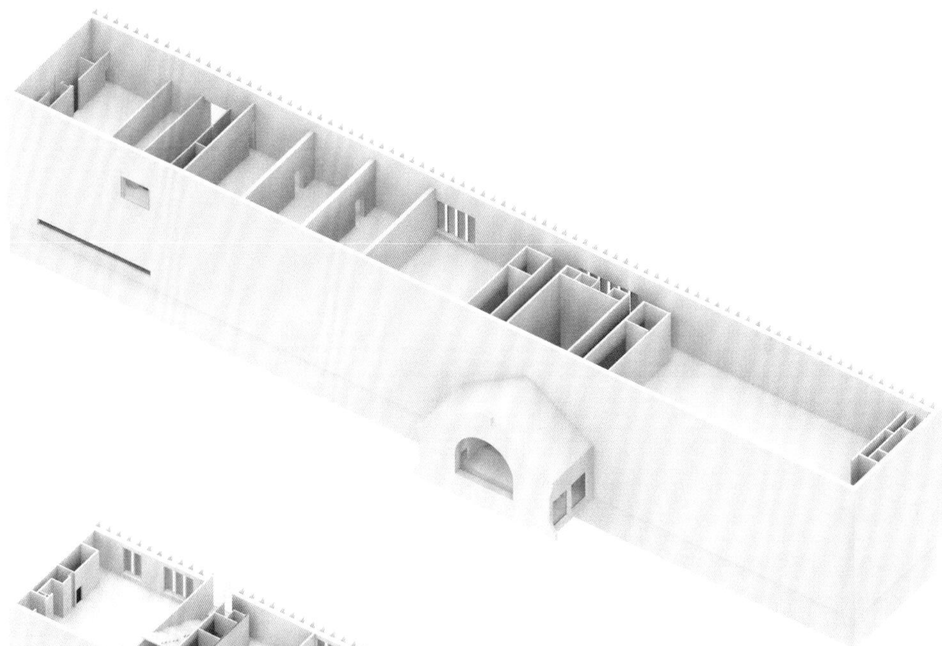

→
First floor

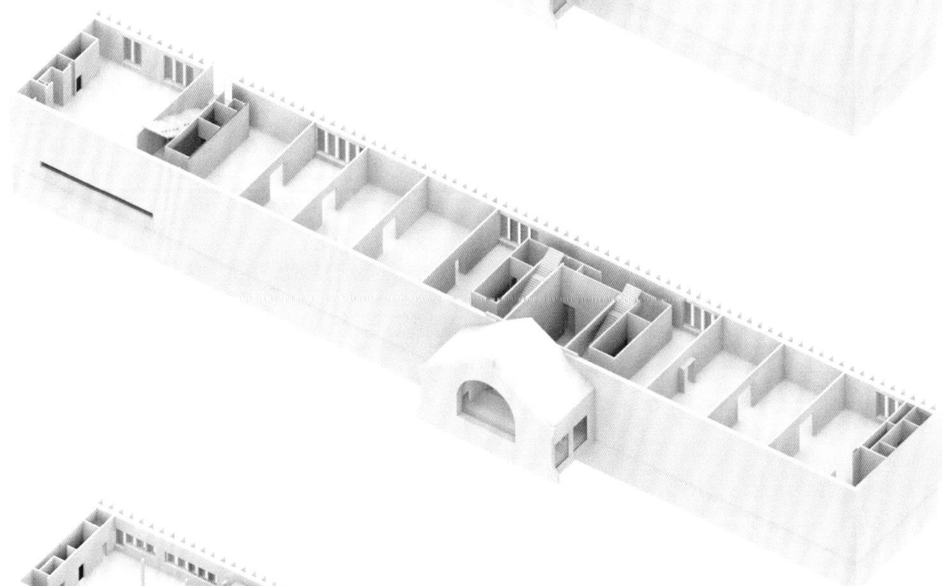

→
Ground floor

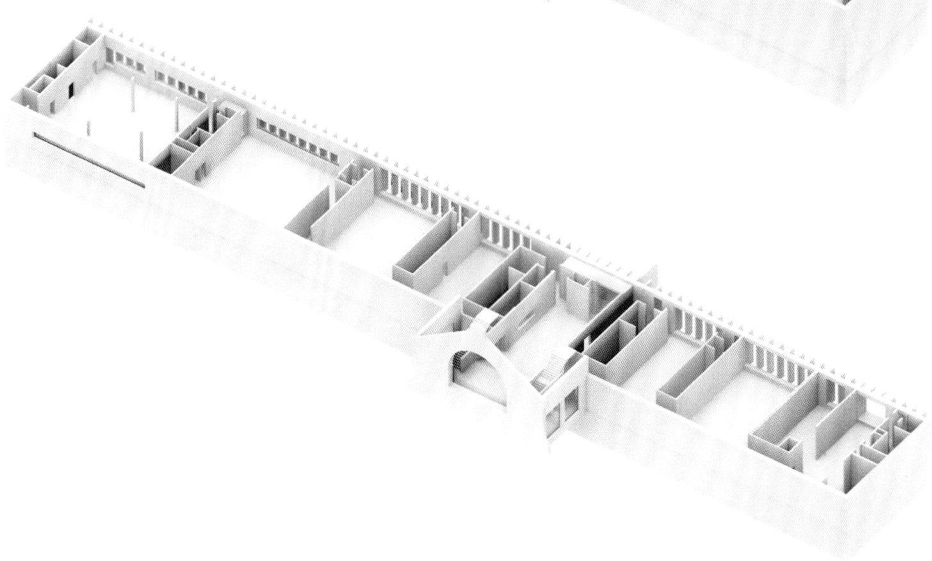

→
South elevation

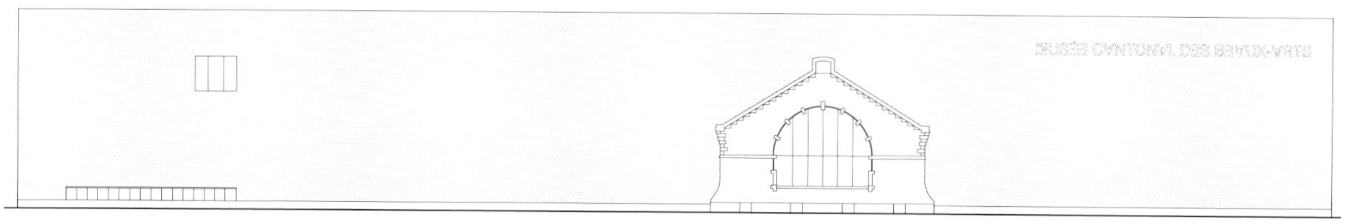

→
North elevation

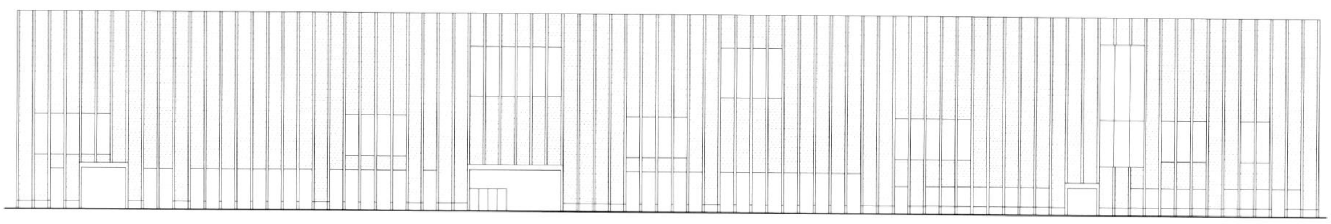

→
East / west elevations

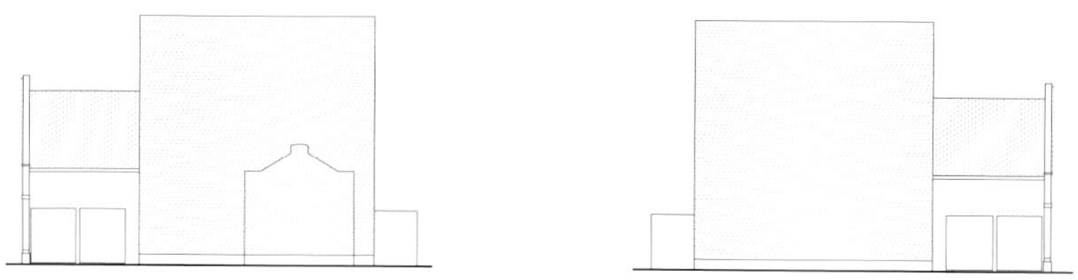

→
Section

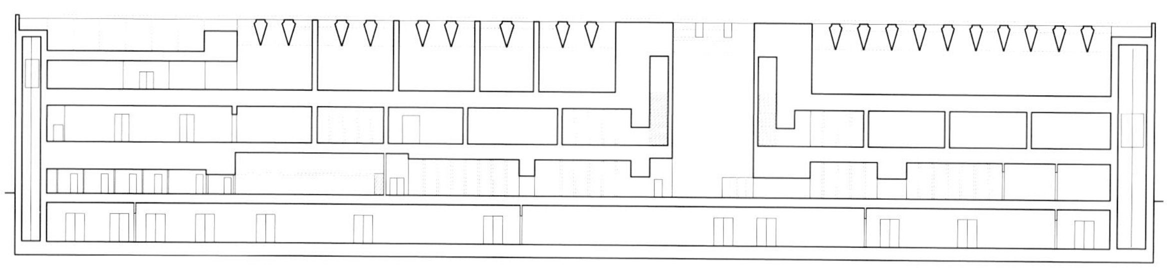

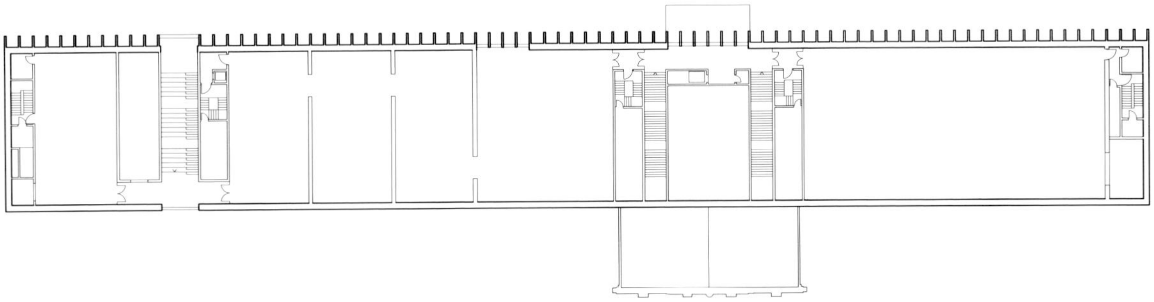

→ Second floor

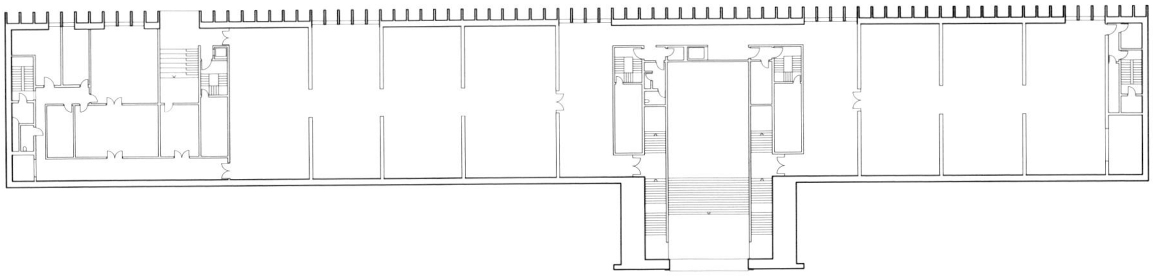

→ First floor

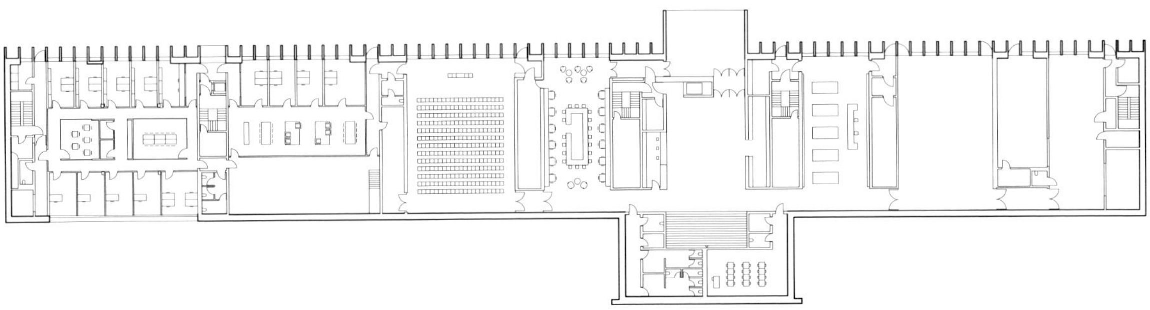

→ Ground floor

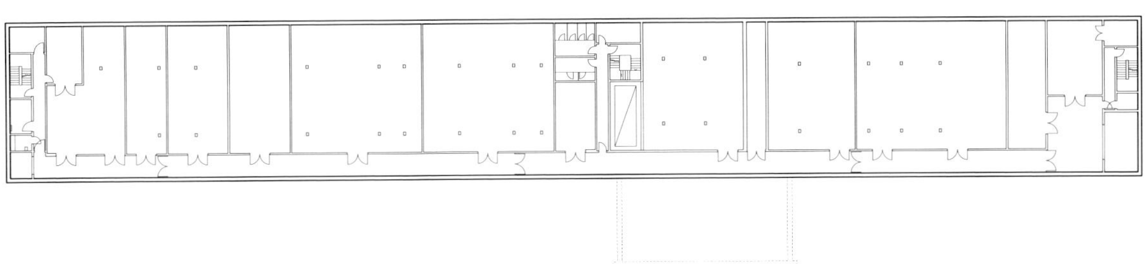

→ Basement

Acknowledgments

We would like to thank all those who made the creation of the new Museum of Fine Arts on the PLATFORM 10 site feasible, and without whom this project would not have been possible.

PLATFORM 10
Steering Committee (06.01.2019)
Cesla Amarelle
Pascal Broulis
Stéphane Droux
Pierre-Antoine Hildbrand
Grégoire Junod
Natacha Litzistorf
Nicole Minder
Bernard Pittet
Philippe Pont

MCBA
Authorized Representatives
Fabrizio Barozzi
Pieter Jansens
Matthieu Troillet
Alberto Veiga
Carlos Viladoms
Léa Zennaf
Bernard Zurbuchen

Directorate General of Buildings and Heritage
Laurent Amez-Droz
Laurent Chenu
Christophe Chopard
Yves Golay
Olivier Michel
Claude Péguiron
Yves Roland Perrin

Directorate of Architecture and Engineering
Frédéric Abbet
Jean Claude Floret
Nicolas Fröhlich
Christopher Pyroth
Jesse Ramandrosoa

Museum of Fine Arts Foundation (06.01.2019)
Olivier Audemars
Bice Curiger
Julien Chapuis
Bernard Decrauzat
Marco Francioli
Nicole Minder
Alfred Pacquement
Cyrille Piguet
Olivier Steimer

The creation of the new Museum of Fine Arts was also able to count on the commitment of many people who provided it with unfailing support. We would also like to express our gratitude to them through these few lines.

Francisco Aires Mateus
Alain Barbey
Félix Baumann
Béatrice Béguin
Nicolas Bideau
Daniel Brélaz
Jean-François Bodin
Geneviève Bonnard
Patrice Bulliard
Thierry Chanard
David Chipperfield
Yves Deillon
Patrick Devanthéry
Raymond Ducrey
Giselle Eberhard-Cotton
Miguel Fernandez-Ruiz
Hartwig Fischer
Olivier Français
Tatyana Franck
Pierre Frey
Florence Germond
Vincent Grandjean
André Hoffmann
Thomas Huber
Christian Jelk
Pierre Keller †
Viviane Keller
Michael Kinzer
Harumi Klossowska de Rola
Setsuko Klossowska de Rola
Stéphane Kropf
Nathalie Luyet
Anne-Catherine Lyon
François Marthaler
Olivier Mosset
Aurelio Mutoni
Yves Noël
Catherine Othenin-Girard
Charles Pictet
Chantal Prod'Hom
Eric Rochat
Yves Roulet
Christine Salvadé
Jean-Luc Spertini
Laurent Staffelbach
Deborah Saunt
Xavier Veilhan
Brigitte Waridel
Elisabeth Wermelinger
Silvia Zamora

The author wishes to thank the following people for their assistance and encouragement in the preparation of this book:

Emmanuel Ventura
Daniel Abimi
Bernard Fibicher
Fabrizio Barozzi and Alberto Veiga
Flavia Cocchi
Nicolas Fröhlich
Nora Rupp

Benefactors

Fondation Les Mûrons
Loterie Romande
Fondation Anita et Werner Damm-Etienne
Fondation Leenaards
Audemars Piguet
Banque Cantonale Vaudoise
Fondation Gandur pour l'Art
Alice Pauli
Fondation Ernst Göhner
Fondation Art et Vie
Nestlé
Philip Morris International Management SA
Etablissement cantonal d'assurance contre l'incendie et les éléments naturels
Fondation Payot pour la promotion de la lecture et l'accès à la culture en Suisse romande
Association rétrospective Pierrette Gonseth-Favre

Credits

ARTWORK CREDITS

p. 014
Marc-Louis Arlaud (Orbe, 1772–Lausanne, 1845)
Self-Portrait, 1837
Oil on canvas, 60 × 49.5 cm (23.6 × 19.5 inches)
Museum of Fine Arts, Lausanne
Donation of the artist, 1842. Inv. 766
© MCBA

pp. 016–017
Friedrich von Martens (Venice, 1806–Paris, 1885)
Place de la Riponne and the Arlaud Museum, c. 1850
Etching, 12.1 × 17.3 cm (4.7 × 6.8 inches)
© Collection of Musée historique Lausanne

p. 018
Gaspard André (Lyon, 1840–Cannes, 1896)
Design for the main entrance of the Palais de Rumine, 1890
Drawing and watercolor, 100 × 100 cm (39.4 × 39.4 inches)
Lausanne City Archives, cote: 721/4
© Laurent Dubois, Bibliothèque cantonale
et universitaire de Lausanne

p. 021
Gaspard André (Lyon, 1840–Cannes, 1896)
Taureau Farnèse project for the Palais de Rumine, 1890
Drawing and watercolor, 53.5 × 82 cm (21 × 32.3 inches)
Lausanne City Archives, cote: 721/1
© Laurent Dubois, Bibliothèque cantonale
et universitaire de Lausanne

p. 022
Abraham-Louis-Rodolphe Ducros
(Moudon, 1748–Lausanne, 1810)
Sicile. Orage nocturne à Cefalù
(Sicily. Evening Storm at Cefalù), c. 1800–05
Watercolor, gouache, and oil on paper pasted
on canvas, 96 × 74 cm (37.8 × 29.1 inches)
Museum of Fine Arts, Lausanne
Ducros Collection. Acquisition, 1816. Inv. 812
© MCBA

p. 025
Charles Gleyre (Chevilly, 1806–Paris, 1874)
Esquisse pour L'Exécution du Major Davel
(Sketch for The Execution of Major Davel), 1847–48
Oil on canvas, 40 × 32 cm (15.7 × 12.6 inches)
Museum of Fine Arts, Lausanne
Acquisition, 2012. Inv. 2012-021
© MCBA

pp. 026–027
Charles Gleyre (Chevilly, 1806–Paris, 1874)
Étude pour La Danse des bacchantes
(bacchante couchée) (Study for The Dance of the
Bacchantes—Reclining Bacchante), 1848–49
Black pencil on paper, 27.7 × 44.5 cm (10.9 × 17.5 inches)
Museum of Fine Arts, Lausanne
Acquisition, 1908. Inv. 1096
© MCBA

pp. 028–029
Charles Gleyre (Chevilly, 1806–Paris, 1874)
La Danse des bacchantes (The Dance of the Bacchantes), 1849
Oil on canvas, 147 × 243 cm (57.9 × 95.7 inches)
Museum of Fine Arts, Lausanne
Acquisition with a nonrecurring appropriation from the Etat
de Vaud, the participation of the Fondation Gottfried Keller,
Gonset Holding S.A., Fondation Ernst Göhner, Association
des Amis du Musée, ATAG Ernst & Young, 1995. Inv. 1995-093
© MCBA

p. 031
Théophile-Alexandre Steinlen (Lausanne, 1859–Paris, 1923)
Étude de chat. Carnet Sources-Croquis
(Study of a Cat. Carnet Sources-Croquis), c. 1902
Charcoal on paper, 27 × 20.5 cm (10.6 × 8.1 inches)
Museum of Fine Arts, Lausanne
Acquisition, 1954. Inv. 1754
© MCBA

p. 033
Félix Vallotton (Lausanne, 1865–Paris, 1925)
La Paresse (Laziness), 1896
Wood-block print on paper, no. 18 (one of approximately
180 prints), 25 × 32.5 cm (9.8 × 12.8 inches)
Museum of Fine Arts, Lausanne
Acquisition, 1903. Inv. 1188
© MCBA

pp. 034–035
Félix Vallotton (Lausanne, 1865–Paris, 1925)
La Chambre rouge (The Red Room), 1898
Tempera on cardboard, 50 × 68.5 cm (19.7 × 26.9 inches)
Museum of Fine Arts, Lausanne
Acquisition, 1983. Inv. 1983-067
© MCBA

pp. 038–039
Louis Soutter (Morges, 1871–Ballaigues, 1942)
Souplesse (Suppleness), 1939
Gouache and shoe polish on paper, 44 × 58 cm (17.3 × 22.8 inches)
Museum of Fine Arts, Lausanne
Acquisition, 1957. Inv. 418
© MCBA

p. 041
Ai Wei Wei (Beijing, 1957)
Dragon in Progress, 2013
Bamboo, silk, and Xuan rice paper, 250 × 250 × 180 cm
(98.4 x 98.4 x 70.8 inches)
Exhibition *Ai Wei Wei. D'ailleurs c'est toujours les autres*, 2017–18,
Museum of Fine Arts, Lausanne
© Studio Ai Wei Wei

p. 043
Jacques Sablet (Morges, 1749–Paris, 1803)
Portrait de famille avec le Colisée
(Family Portrait with the Colosseum), 1791
Oil on canvas, 60 × 72 cm (23.6 × 28.3 inches)
Museum of Fine Arts, Lausanne
Deposit of the Fondation Gottfried Keller,
Office fédéral de la culture, Bern, 1932. Inv. 738
© MCBA

p. 044
Auguste Rodin (Paris, 1840–Meudon, 1917)
L'Homme au serpent (The Man with a Serpent), 1885 (cast: 1887)
Bronze, brown patina, 69.5 × 55 × 29 cm (27.4 × 21.6 × 11.4 inches)
Museum of Fine Arts, Lausanne
Anonymous donation, 2015. Inv. 2015-028
© MCBA

p. 045
Ferdinand Hodler (Bern, 1853–Geneva, 1918)
Blick ins Unendliche III (Look into the Infinite III), 1903–04
Oil on canvas, 100 × 80 cm (39.4 × 31.5 inches)
Museum of Fine Arts, Lausanne
Acquisition, 1994. Inv. 1994-032
© MCBA

pp. 046–047
Ferdinand Hodler (Bern, 1853–Geneva, 1918)
Le Lac Léman vu de Chexbres
(Lake Geneva Seen from Chexbres), 1904
Oil on canvas, 70.5 × 108.3 cm (27.6 × 42.6 inches)
Museum of Fine Arts, Lausanne
Acquisition, 1904. Inv. 715
© MCBA

pp. 048–049
Ernest Biéler (Rolle, 1863–Lausanne, 1948)
L'Eau mystérieuse (The Mysterious Water), 1911
Tempera on paper pasted on canvas
146.3 × 376.4 cm (57.5 × 148.2 inches)
Museum of Fine Arts, Lausanne
Deposit of the Fondation Gottfried Keller,
Office fédéral de la culture, Bern, 1913. Inv. 555
© MCBA

p. 050
Alice Bailly (Geneva, 1872–Lausanne, 1938)
Jeu d'éventail ou Femme à l'éventail
(Fan Game, or Woman with a Fan), 1913
Oil on canvas, 92 × 73 cm (36.2 × 28.7 inches)
Museum of Fine Arts, Lausanne
Acquisition, 1997. Inv. 1997-093
© MCBA

p. 051
Balthus (Balthazar Klossowski de Rola)
(Paris, 1908–Rossinière, 2001)
Le Roi des chats (The King of Cats), 1935
Oil on canvas, 78 × 49.7 cm (30.7 × 19.5 inches)
Museum of Fine Arts, Lausanne
Donation of the Fondation
Balthus Klossowski de Rola, 2016. Inv. 2016-048
© 2019 Balthus

pp. 052–053
Paul Klee (Münchenbuchsee, 1879–Locarno, 1940)
Am Nil (On the Nile), 1939
Distemper paint on paper mounted on jute
75 × 125 cm (29.5 × 49.2 inches)
Museum of Fine Arts, Lausanne
Donation, 2011. Inv. 2011-200
© MCBA

pp. 054–055
Aloïse Blanche Corbaz (Lausanne, 1886–Gimel, 1964)
Bonne année (recto) *(Happy New Year)*, 4th period: 1951–60
Colored crayon on paper, 52.8 × 84.1 cm (20.8 × 33.1 inches)
Museum of Fine Arts, Lausanne
Donation of Professor Hans Steck, 1971. Inv. 1971-041
All rights reserved

pp. 056–057
Bruce Nauman (Fort Wayne, 1941)
Untitled (Hand Circle), 1996
Bronze, 12,7 × 67,3 × 63,5 cm (5 × 26.5 25 inches)
Museum of Fine Arts, Lausanne
Acquisition with the support of a friend
of the arts, 1996. Inv. 1997-003
© Bruce Nauman / 2019, ProLitteris, Zurich

pp. 058–059
Anselm Kiefer (Donaueschingen, 1945)
Die Rheintöchter (The Rhine Daughters), 1982–2013
Collage of wood-block prints, acrylic and varnish on canvas
190 × 330 × 5.5 cm (74.8 × 129.9 × 2.1 inches)
Museum of Fine Arts, Lausanne
Donation of Alice Pauli, 2016. Inv. 2017-004
© Anselm Kiefer

pp. 060–061
Philippe Decrauzat (Lausanne, 1974)
Untitled, 2001
Acrylic on canvas, 140 × 245 cm (55.1 × 96.4 inches)
Museum of Fine Arts, Lausanne
Acquisition of the Commission cantonale
des activités culturelles, 2002. Inv. 2002-004
© MCBA

p. 158
Giuseppe Penone (Garessio, 1947)
Luce e ombra (Light and Shadow), 2011
Bronze, gold leaf, and granite
1,450 × 470 × 490 cm (570.9 × 185 × 192.9 inches)
Museum of Fine Arts, Lausanne
Donation of Alice Pauli, 2016. Inv. 2017-006
© 2019, ProLitteris, Zurich

p. 166
Pierre Soulages (Rodez, 1919)
Peinture, 324 × 362 cm (Polyptyque J), 1987
Oil on canvas, 324 × 362 cm (127.5 × 142.5 inches)
Museum of Fine Arts, Lausanne
Donation of Alice Pauli, 2017. Inv. 1999-063
© 2019, ProLitteris, Zurich

p. 196
Dimitri Bähler (Moutier, 1988)
Small Oblong Plate
(Fur Patterns / Black on White Satin), 2013
Ceramic, 26 × 20 × 2.5 cm (10.2 × 7.9 × 1 inches)
© Collection of mudac

p. 198
Pieke Bergmans (Sprang Capelle, 1978)
Light Bulb (chair), 2015
Glass, metal, and LED, 83 × 42 × 40 cm
(32.7 × 16.5 × 15.7 inches)
© Collection of mudac

p. 199
Hans Steiner (Bern, 1907–62)
Piscine KaWeDe, Berne
(KaWeDe Swimming Pool, Bern), 1935–40
Gelatin silver bromide print
19.5 × 17.5 cm (7.6 × 6.8 inches)
© Musée de l'Elysée, Lausanne

PHOTO CREDITS

© Aires Mateus
p. 194

© Manuel Aires Mateus
p. 192

© Yves André
pp. 068, 070–071, 074–077, 098–103, 116–117, 213–215

© Jesus Arenas
pp. 104–113

© Iwan Baan
p. 090

© Fabrizio Barozzi
p. 150

© Barozzi Veiga
p. 087

© Barozzi Veiga / MIR
p. 086

© BBK Architekten
pp. 064, 067

© Chloé Bellemère
p. 183

© Enzyme Design
p. 186

© Matthieu Gafsou
pp. 122–123, 125–126, 130–132, 134–138, 140–149, 156, 158,
172–177, 181, 184–185, 202, 206–207, 210–211, back cover

© Laurian Ghinitoiu
p. 082

© Stefano Grazioni
p. 093

© Hufton & Crow
p. 094

© José Hevia
p. 081

© Simon Menges
Cover, pp. 083, 118–121, 127–129, 133, 139

© Raphaëlle Mueller
p. 196

© Benoît Peverelli
p. 06

© Jean-Bernard Sieber
p. 212

Museum of Fine Arts, Lausanne:
Architecture, Art

First published in the United States of America in 2019
by Rizzoli International Publications, Inc.
300 Park Avenue South
New York, NY 10010, USA
www.rizzoliusa.com

Texts
Philip Jodidio
Foreword
Robert Wilson

Publisher
Charles Miers
Editorial Director
Catherine Bonifassi
Art Direction
Atelier Flavia Cocchi
Editor
Victorine Lamothe
Production Director
Maria Pia Gramaglia
Managing Editor
Lynn Scrabis

Editorial Coordination
CASSI EDITION
Vanessa Blondel
Lili Doillon
Harriet Graham

Printed in Italy

2019 2020 2021 2022 / 10 9 8 7 6 5 4 3 2 1

ISBN: 978-0-8478-6587-1
Library of Congress Control Number: 2019944346

Visit us online: Facebook.com/RizzoliNewYork
Twitter: @Rizzoli_Books
Instagram.com/RizzoliBooks
Pinterest.com/RizzoliBooks
Youtube.com/user/RizzoliNY
Issuu.com/Rizzoli